A NEW
WORLDLY
ORDER

A NEW WORLDLY ORDER

John Paul II and Human Freedom

Edited by George Weigel

ETHICS AND PUBLIC POLICY CENTER

Library of Congress Cataloging-in-Publication Data

A New Wordly Order : John Paul II and Human Freedom /
edited by George Weigel.
p.   cm.
Includes index.
1. Catholic Church. Pope (1978- : John Paul II). Centesimus annus.
2. Catholic Church—Doctrines.   3. Sociology, Christian (Catholic)
4. Freedom (Theology)   5. Church and social problems—Catholic Church.
I. Weigel, George.
BX1753.N49   1991   261.8—dc20   91-862 CIP

ISBN 0–89633–170–9 (cloth, alk. paper)
ISBN 0–89633–171–7 (paper, alk paper)

Distributed by arrangement with:

National Book Network
4720 Boston Way
Lanham, MD 20706

3 Henrietta Street
London WC2E 8LU England

All Ethics and Public Policy Center books are produced on acid-free paper. The paper used in this publication meets the minimum requirements of American National Standard for Information Sciences—Permanence of Paper for Printed Library Materials, ANSI Z39.48–1984.   ∞ ™

Ethics and Public Policy Center
1015 Fifteenth Street N.W.
Washington, D.C. 20005
(202) 682–1200

Contents

Preface

IT wasn't supposed to happen like this. One hundred years ago, not even the most fervent Catholic would have predicted that an encyclical letter by the Bishop of Rome, at the end of the twentieth century, would be front-page news in virtually all the world's major newspapers, the subject of intense scholarly debate among evangelical and liberal Protestants, Jews, and Catholics, and a matter of considerable interest to corporate executives, trade union leaders, and government officials. And yet that is precisely what happened in May 1991 when Pope John Paul II issued the encyclical *Centesimus Annus* ("The Hundredth Year") to mark the centenary of Pope Leo XIII's *Rerum Novarum* and to set the future intellectual direction of Catholic social teaching.

Why?

The personal magnetism and moral authority of John Paul II are surely among the reasons why. Thirteen years into his Petrine ministry as "servant of the servants of God," John Paul II commands an audience far beyond the formal boundaries of the Roman Catholic Church (itself, of course, a communion of almost a billion members). When John Paul II speaks, people listen. They might not always agree, but they listen. This pope speaks to, and on behalf of, the human family in a way that no other world figure can hope to match. What he says about worldly things—about culture, politics, and economics, about "Real Socialism" and "the new capitalism"—matters.

Centesimus Annus also drew intense attention in the days after its publication because many commentators, from across the religious and political spectrums, sensed that the world was at something of a turning point and, moreover, a turning point defined in large part by profound religious and moral convictions. The Revolution of 1989 in Central and Eastern Europe, the churnings in the world's last empire (soon to give birth to the astonishing New Russian Revolution of August 1991), the democratic transitions in Latin America and East Asia: all these seemed to embody in bold, even world-historical terms the truth of the biblical teaching that man does not live by bread alone. Across an extraordinarily wide span of the world's population, courageous men and women were saying "No" to ancient and modern tyrannies, and precisely on the basis of a higher and more compelling "Yes." The springtime of nations of the late 1980s and early 1990s was born in no small part out of what seemed to be a revolution of the spirit.

What would John Paul II, himself a major actor in the democratic drama of Central and Eastern Europe, have to say about all of this? Could he help define a new worldly order, one that was built on the foundations of human freedom and human solidarity and yet avoided the utopian (and totalitarian) temptations that had beset the world since Rousseau and his disciples had tried to make all things new through politics?

Centesimus Annus touches on virtually every aspect of public life at the end of the twentieth century. But, this being the age of the sound-bite, the debate over the encyclical was far too short-lived. This book is an attempt to reignite and deepen that discussion and, perhaps more importantly, to keep it lively and vigorous beyond the worlds of internal Catholic argument so that the pope's address to "all men and women of good will" might be more fully engaged.

In the pages that follow, a condensation of the encyclical is preceded by a reflection on the letter by its author, whose comments on just what it is he thought he was doing surely merit close attention. Twenty-one commentators—social scientists, theologians, political theorists, lawyers, and journalists; conservatives, neo-conservatives, and liberals; Jews, Protestants, and Catholics; Americans and Europeans—then offer their distinctive analyses of *Centesimus Annus*. Not all of them are wholly complimentary. But disagreement does not imply disrespect, and the moral deliberation for which *Centesimus Annus* so eloquently calls is surely enhanced by what the diplomats call a "free and frank exchange of views." In that spirit, my colleague Robert Royal concludes the volume by reminding us that the conversation intensified by the encyclical is an open-ended one, in which reflection on the reference points provided by John Paul II may lead in surprising directions.

I should like to thank Carol Griffith, Christopher Ditzenberger, and Gretchen Baudhuin of the Ethics and Public Policy Center staff, and our friends and colleagues at University Press of America, for their good work in bringing this volume quickly to fruition. Thanks, too, to those who gave us permission to bring previously published material to what we hope will be a wide, ecumenical, and international audience.

GEORGE WEIGEL

Washington, D.C.
The Feast of St. Augustine, 1991

Prologue

The New 'New Things'

GEORGE WEIGEL

THE social encyclical issued by Pope John Paul II in May 1991 is a landmark event in contemporary religious thought about human freedom and its embodiment in culture, economics, and politics. Written to honor the centenary of *Rerum Novarum*, the 1891 letter of Pope Leo XIII that began the papal tradition of modern Catholic social teaching, *Centesimus Annus* ("The Hundredth Year") is both a look back at the *res novae*, the "new things" that seized the attention of Leo XIII, and a look ahead at what we might call the "new 'new things,'" the new facts of public life at the end of the twentieth century and the turn of the third Christian millennium. Like other papal documents, *Centesimus Annus* reaffirms the classic themes of Catholic social thought. But it is John Paul II's creative extension of the tradition that makes this encyclical a singularly bold document, one that is likely to redraw the boundaries of the Catholic debate over the right-ordering of culture, economics, and politics for the foreseeable future.

Centesimus Annus is not, however, a matter of Catholic inside baseball. The encyclical addresses itself to "all men and women of good will." Moreover, scholars and religious leaders outside the formal boundaries of Roman Catholicism have shown an increasing interest in modern Catholic social teaching as perhaps the most well-developed and coherent set of

1

Christian reference points for conducting the public argument about how we should order our lives, loves, and loyalties in society today. (Curiously enough, John Paul II is sometimes more appreciated as a witness to Christian orthodoxy outside his church than within it: as a prominent Southern Baptist put it to a group of Catholic colleagues in early 1991, "Down where I come from, people are saying, 'You folks finally got yourself a pope who knows how to pope.' ")

Centesimus Annus should be of special interest to Americans. For better or for worse—and usually for both—the United States is the testbed for modernity, and for whatever-it-is that's going to come after modernity. We are the world's only superpower, and we are a superpower whose moral *raison d'être* is freedom. As a nation "conceived in liberty," and as the leader of the party of freedom in world politics, the United States ought to pay careful attention to what the most influential moral leader in the contemporary world has to say about the many dimensions of freedom, and about the intimate relation between freedom and truth: particularly the "truth about man," which has been such a prominent theme in the teaching of John Paul II since his election in 1987.

Speaking in Miami in September 1987, the pope described the United States in these terms:

> Among the many admirable values of this nation there is one that stands out in particular. It is freedom. The concept of freedom is part of the very fabric of this nation as a political community of free people. Freedom is a great gift, a great blessing of God.
>
> From the beginning of America, freedom was directed to forming a well-ordered society and to promoting its peaceful life. Freedom was channeled to the fullness of human life, to the preservation of human dignity, and to the safeguarding of all human rights. An experience of ordered freedom is truly a part of the cherished history of this land.
>
> This is the freedom that America is called to live and

guard and to transmit. She is called to exercise it in such a way that it will also benefit the cause of freedom in other nations and among other peoples. The only true freedom, the only freedom that can truly satisfy, is the freedom to do what we ought as human beings created by God according to his plan. It is the freedom to live the truth of what we are and who we are before God, the truth of our identity as children of God, as brothers and sisters in a common humanity. That is why Jesus Christ linked truth and freedom together, stating solemnly, "You will know the truth and the truth will set you free" (John 8:32). All people are called to recognize the liberating truth of the sovereignty of God over them as individuals and as nations.

So much for the image of John-Paul-the-Polish-authoritarian, so assiduously propounded by the prestige press (and by the party of dissent in American Catholicism). The truth of the matter is precisely the opposite: were one to hang a moniker on this remarkable Bishop of Rome, one might well call him the "Pope of Freedom."

What John Paul II means by "freedom," of course, is not precisely what America's cultural elites have had in mind since the fevered "liberations" of the 1960s. And so an argument is engaged: What is this freedom that is a "great gift, a great blessing of God"? How is it to be lived by free men and women, in free societies that must protect individual liberty while concurrently advancing the common good?

Enter *Centesimus Annus*.

THE TRUTH ABOUT MAN

Viewed most comprehensively, *Centesimus Annus* is a profound meditation on human nature, on man's quest for a freedom that will truly satisfy the deepest yearnings of the human heart. John Paul II regards that human search for true freedom as something "built in" to the very nature of man's way of being in the world, and "built in" precisely by a God whom we are to find, and worship, in freedom.

The "Problem" of Freedom

Centesimus Annus begins with a review of the teaching of Leo XIII in *Rerum Novarum*. For there, in 1891, the Church began to grapple with the new problem of freedom that had been created by the upheavals of the Industrial Revolution (in economics) and the French Revolution (in politics). "Traditional society was passing away and another was beginning to be formed—one which brought the hope of new freedoms but also the threat of new forms of injustice and servitude." That threat was particularly grave when modernity ignored "the essential bond between human freedom and truth." Leo XIII understood, his successor argues, that a "freedom which refused to be bound to the truth would fall into arbitrariness and end up submitting itself to the vilest of passions, to the point of self-destruction." In the last decade of this bloodiest of centuries, it is difficult to suggest that Leo XIII was prematurely pessimistic about certain aspects of the modern quest for freedom.

From Leo XIII on, Catholic social teaching's "answer" to the "problem" of freedom has begun with a moral reflection on man himself, and an insistence on the dignity and worth of each individual human being as a creature endowed with intelligence and will, and thus made "in the image and likeness of God." Therefore the beginning of the answer to the rapaciousness of Manchesterian liberalism in economics was "the dignity of the worker . . . [and] the dignity of work." And the beginning of the answer to the massive repression and injustice of twentieth-century tyrannies was Leo XIII's insistence on the "necessary limits to the state's intervention in human affairs." Why are those limits "necessary"? Because "the individual, the family, and society are prior to the State, and . . .

the State exists in order to protect their rights and not stifle them."

The Catholic human rights revolution of the late twentieth century thus owes a debt of gratitude to the last pope of the nineteenth century, Leo XIII, for it was Leo who first posed Christian *personalism* as the alternative to socialist collectivism (which subsumed human personality into the mass) and to radical individualism (which locked human personality into a self-made prison of solipsism). John Paul II, from the moment he took office in October 1978, has been a vigorous proponent of basic human rights, particularly the fundamental right of religious freedom. This pattern continues in *Centesimus Annus*, in which the pope decries the situation in those countries "which covertly, or even openly, deny to citizens of faiths other than that of the majority the full exercise of their civil and religious rights, preventing them from taking part in the cultural process, and restricting both the Church's right to preach the Gospel and the right of those who hear this preaching to accept it."

"Rights": Deepening the Debate

For that reason, it is all the more striking that the human rights language is a bit more muted in *Centesimus Annus* than in John Paul's earlier encyclicals—and far more muted than it was in Pope John XXIII's *Pacem in Terris*. The pope has not lost any interest in the problems of human rights. Rather, he now seems determined to deepen (and, in some respects, to discipline) the debate over "rights" by linking rights to *obligations* and to *truth*.

On this latter point, conscience is not a kind of moral free agent, in which an "autonomous self" declares something to be right because it is right "for me." No, conscience is "bound to the truth." And the truth about man is not to be confused with "an appeal to the appetites and inclinations toward immediate gratification," an appeal that is "utilitarian" in character and does not reflect "the hierarchy of the true values of human existence."

Nor are "rights" simply a matter of our immunities from the coercive power of others, important as such immunities are: rights exist so that we can fulfill our obligations. Thus a man should be free economically so that he can enter into more cooperative relationships with others, and meet his obligations to work in order to "provide for the needs of his family, his community, his nation, and ultimately all humanity." Ownership, too, has its obligations: "Just as the person fully realizes himself in the free gift of self, so too ownership morally satisfies itself in the creation, at the proper time and in the proper way, of opportunities for work and human growth for all."

By hearkening back to the Christian personalism of Leo XIII, while at the same time "thickening" the concept of "rights" in the Catholic tradition, John Paul II has, in *Centesimus Annus*, provided a powerful example of Christian anthropology at its finest. But this is no abstract philosophical exercise. For having set the proper framework for thinking about public life, the pope immediately brings his analysis of the "truth about man" to bear on the Revolution of 1989 in Central and Eastern Europe.

REVOLUTION OF THE SPIRIT

The fundamental error of socialism is anthropological in nature. Socialism considers the individual person simply as an element, a molecule within the social organism, so that the good of the individual is completely subordinated to the functioning of the socio-economic mechanism. Socialism likewise maintains that the good of the individual can be realized without reference to his free choice, to the unique and exclusive responsibility he exercises in the face of good or evil. Man is thus reduced to a series of social relationships, and the concept of the person as the . . . subject of moral decision disappears, the very subject whose decisions build the social order.

From this mistaken conception of the person there arise both a distortion of law . . . and an opposition to private property. A person who is deprived of something he can call "his own," and of the possibility of earning a living through his own initiative, comes to depend on the social machine and on those who control it. This makes it much more difficult for him to recognize his dignity as a person, and hinders progress toward the building up of an authentic human community.—CENTESIMUS ANNUS, 13

Western political scientists and international-relations specialists have had a hard time figuring out just what happened in Central and Eastern Europe in 1989. "Delayed modernization" seems to be the preferred answer from the ivory tower: the economic systems of the Communist world couldn't compete, and the only way to change them was to get rid of the political regimes that had imposed collectivism in the first place. It is, in truth, a deliciously Marxist "answer" to the utter collapse of Marxism—and a worrisome indication of how deeply quasi-Marxist themes have sunk into the collective unconscious of the new knowledge class.

Pope John Paul II, for one, isn't buying any of this.

Centesimus Annus is well worth careful study for its marvelous third chapter alone. For in "The Year 1989," the pope offers a succinct, pointed, and persuasive analysis of the roots of the Revolution of 1989. The fundamental problem with Communism, or "Real Socialism," was not its economic decrepitude. Rather, Communism failed because it denied "the truth about man." Communism's failures were first and foremost moral failures. "The God That Failed" was a false god whose acolytes led societies and economies into terminal crisis.

Yalta Revisited

Pope John Paul begins his historical analysis of 1989 in 1945, with the Yalta Agreements. "Yalta," in fact, looms very large indeed in the vision of the Polish pontiff. The Second World War, "which should have re-established freedom and restored the right of nations, ended without having attained these goals"—indeed, it ended with "the spread of Communist totalitarianism over more than half of Europe and over other parts of the world." Yalta, in other words, was more than a political decision; it was a moral catastrophe and a betrayal of the sacrifices of the war, a betrayal rooted in incomprehension of the nature of Marxist-Leninist totalitarianism.

A failure of moral intuition led to a failure of politics. And thus the first truth about Central and Eastern Europe was that the "Yalta arrangement" could not be regarded as merely a historical datum with which one had to deal. Dealing had to be done (not for nothing did Pope John Paul grow up under the tutelage of Cardinal Stefan Wyszynski of Warsaw, a tenacious primate who gained the Church crucial breathing room in the 1950s). But there should be no illusions. The only "dealing" that would contribute to a genuine peace was a dealing based on the conviction that no peace worthy of the name could be built on the foundations of Yalta.

As it began, so would it end. The origins of this bizarre and, in the pope's terms, "suffocating" empire found their parallels, forty-four years later, in the ways in which the empire fell.

The moral catastrophe of Yalta was attacked at its roots by "the Church's commitment to defend and promote human rights," by a confrontation with Stalin's empire at the level of ethics, history, and culture. Communism, and particularly Communist atheism, the pope said time and again, was "an act against man." And the antidote to the false humanism of Marxism-Leninism would come from a truly Christian humanism in which men and women once again learned the human dignity that was theirs by birthright.

1979: A Return to Poland

That understanding had never been completely snuffed out in Central and Eastern Europe. But there was fear. And it seems in retrospect that the people of the region—first in Poland, and then elsewhere—began to face down their fear during John Paul II's first, dramatic return to Poland in June 1979. His message during that extraordinary pilgrimage was decidedly "pre-political." It was a message about ethics, culture, and history devoted to explicating "the truth about man" that Poles knew in their bones—the truth that their regime had denied for two generations. It was not a message about "politics" in the narrow sense of the struggle for power. But it was high-octane Politics in the more venerable sense of the term: as the ongoing argument about the good person, the good society, and the structure of freedom. And that upper-case Politics led, over time, to the distinctive lower-case politics of the Revolution of 1989, the revolution that reversed Yalta.

John Paul II believes that, among the "many factors involved in the fall of [these] oppressive regimes, some deserve special mention." The first point at which "the truth about man" intersected with lower-case "politics" was on the question of the rights of workers. The pope is quite willing to drive home the full irony of the situation:

> It cannot be forgotten that the fundamental crisis of systems claiming to express the rule and indeed the dictatorship of the working class began with the great upheavals which took place in Poland in the name of solidarity. It was the throngs of working people which foreswore the ideology which presumed to speak in their name. On the basis of a hard, lived experience of work and of oppression, it was they who recovered and, in a sense, rediscovered the content and principles of the Church's social doctrine.

That reappropriation of "the truth about man" led to another of the distinctive elements of the Revolution of 1989:

its non-violence. Tactical considerations surely played a role in the choice of non-violence by what we used to call "dissidents": the bad guys had all the guns, and the good guys knew it. But it is hard to explain why the mass of the people remained non-violent—particularly given the glorification of armed revolt in Polish history and culture—unless one understands that a moral revolution preceded the political revolution of 1989.

Other Factors in the Fall

The pope is aware that the economic systems of Central and Eastern Europe were in a shambles by the mid-1980s, and that this played a role in the collapse of Stalin's empire. But he also urges us to consider the economic disaster of command economies, not as a "technical problem" alone, but rather as "a consequence of the violation of the human rights to private initiative, to ownership of property, and to freedom in the economic sector." Marxist economics, just like Leninist politics, refused to acknowledge "the truth about man."

State atheism in the Eastern bloc also carried the seeds of its own destruction, according to John Paul. The "spiritual void" the state created by building a world without windows or doors "deprived the younger generation of direction and in many cases led them, in the irrepressible search for personal identity and for the meaning of life, to rediscover the religious roots of their national cultures, and to rediscover the person of Christ himself as the existentially adequate response to the desire in every human heart for goodness, truth, and life." The Communists had thought they could "uproot the need for God from the human heart." They learned that "it is not possible to succeed in this without throwing the heart into turmoil."

And Communism onto the ash heap of history.

John Paul II's carefully crafted discussion of the Revolution of 1989 makes no claims for the Church's role as agent of the revolution that will strike a fair-minded reader as implausible or excessive. Nor is the Holy See unaware of the many other factors that conspired to produce the peaceful demolition of Stalin's empire: the Helsinki process, which publicly indicted Communist regimes for their human rights violations and created a powerful network of rights activists on both sides of the Iron Curtain; the fact of Mikhail Gorbachev; and SDI, which any number of Vatican officials consider, privately, to have been decisive in forcing a change in Soviet policy.

But John Paul II is determined to teach a more comprehensive truth about the Revolution of 1989: that a revolution of the spirit, built on the sure foundation of "the truth about man," preceded the transfer of power from Communist to democratic hands. The Revolution of 1989, viewed through this wide-angle lens, began in 1979. It was a revolution in which people learned first to throw off fear, and only then to throw off their chains—non-violently. It was a revolution of conservation, in which people reclaimed their moral, cultural, and historical identities. It was, in short, a revolution from "the bottom up"—the bottom, in this case, being the taproots of the historic ethical and cultural self-understandings of individuals and nations.

THE FREE ECONOMY

Not only is it wrong from the ethical point of view to disregard human nature, which is made for freedom, but in practice it is impossible to do so. Where society is so organized as to reduce arbitrarily or even suppress the sphere in which freedom is legitimately exercised, the result is that the life of society becomes progressively disorganized and goes into decline.

Moreover, man, who was created for freedom, bears within himself the wound of original sin, which constantly draws him toward evil and puts him in need of redemption. Not only is this doctrine an integral part of Christian revelation; it also has great hermeneutical value insofar as it helps one to understand human reality. Man tends towards good, but he is also capable of evil. He can transcend his immediate interest and still remain bound to it.

The social order will be all the more stable, the more it takes this fact into account and does not place in opposition personal interest and the interests of society as a whole, but rather seeks to bring them into a fruitful harmony. In fact, when self-interest is violently suppressed, it is replaced by a burdensome system of bureaucratic control which dries up the wellsprings of initiative and creativity. When people think they possess the secret of a perfect social organization which makes evil impossible, they also think that they can use any means, including violence and deceit, in order to bring that organization into being. Politics then becomes a "secular religion" which operates under the illusion of creating paradise in this world. But no political society . . . can ever be confused with the Kingdom of God.—CENTESIMUS ANNUS, 25

Pope John Paul II does not hesitate to draw out the implications of his Christian anthropology of human freedom, and his analysis of the dynamics of the Revolution of 1989, in the field of economics: *Centesimus Annus* contains the most striking papal endorsement of the "free economy" in a century. The endorsement comes in the form of the answer to a pressing question:

Can it be said that, after the failure of Communism, capitalism is the victorious social system, and that capitalism should be the goal of the countries now making efforts to rebuild their economy and society? Is this the model which ought to be proposed to the countries of the Third World which are searching for the path to true economic and civil progress?

The answer is obviously complex. If by "capitalism" is meant an economic system which recognizes the fundamental and positive role of business, the market, private property, and the resulting responsibility for the means of production, as well as free human creativity in the economic sector, then the answer is certainly in the affirmative, even though it would perhaps be more appropriate to speak of a "business economy," "market economy," or simply "free economy." But if by "capitalism" is meant a system in which freedom in the economic sector is not circumscribed within a strong juridical framework which places it at the service of human freedom in its totality, and which sees it as a particular aspect of that freedom, the core of which is ethical and religious, then the reply is certainly negative.

In other words, if by "capitalism" is meant what the West at its best means by capitalism—a tripartite system in which democratic politics and a vibrant culture discipline and temper the free market—then that is the system the pope urges the new democracies and the Third World to adopt, because that is the system most likely to sustain a human freedom that is truly liberating.

Some Striking Points

The defenders of the liberal status quo have insisted that this endorsement carries a lot of conditions with it. Well, of course it does. No thoughtful defender of the market will deny the need for its careful regulation by law, culture, and public morality. What is striking about *Centesimus Annus* comes in passages like these:

- The modern business economy has positive aspects. Its basis is human freedom exercised in the economic field, just as it is exercised in many other fields.

- It is precisely the ability to foresee both the needs of others and the combinations of productive factors most adapted to satisfying those needs that constitutes another important source of wealth in modern society. Besides, many goods cannot be adequately produced through the work of an isolated individual; they require the cooperation of many people in working towards a common goal. Organizing such a productive effort, planning its duration in time, making sure that it corresponds in a positive way to the demands which it must satisfy, and taking the necessary risks—all this too is a source of wealth in today's society. In this way, the role of disciplined and creative human work and, as an essential part of that work, initiative and entrepreneurial ability becomes increasingly evident and decisive.

- Another task of the State is that of overseeing and directing the exercise of human rights in the economic sector. However, primary responsibility in this area belongs not to the State but to individuals and to the various groups and associations which make up society. The State could not directly ensure the right to work for all its citizens unless it controlled every aspect of economic life and restricted the free initiative of individuals.

- Indeed, besides the earth, man's principal resource is man himself.

Centesimus Annus thus marks a decisive break with the curious materialism that has characterized aspects of modern Catholic social teaching since Leo XIII. Wealth-creation today, John Paul II readily acknowledges, has more to do with human creativity and imagination, and with political and economic systems capable of unleashing that creativity and imagination, than with "resources" *per se*. And that, John Paul II seems to suggest, is one of the "signs of the times" to which Catholic social thought must be attentive.

An Empirical View of the "Option"

In fact, one of the distinctive characteristics of *Centesimus Annus* is its empirical sensitivity. John Paul II has thought carefully about what does and what doesn't work in exercising a "preferential option for the poor" in the new democracies, in the Third World, and in impoverished parts of the developed world. The "preferential option," the pope seems to suggest, is a formal principle: its content should be determined, not on the basis of ideological orthodoxy (that's what was rejected in the Revolution of 1989), but by empirical facts. And as far as this pope seems concerned, the evidence is in. What works best for the poor is democratic polities and properly regulated market economies. Why? Because democracy and the market are the systems that best cohere with human nature, with human freedom, with "the truth about man."

It will take some time for this new departure in Catholic social thought to be digested by those committed to what the pope calls the "impossible compromise between Marxism and Christianity," as well as by those who continue to search for a chimerical Catholic "third way" between capitalism and socialism. (At a meeting in Rome shortly after the encyclical was published, for example, the dean of the social-science faculty at the Pontifical Gregorian University told me that "Capitalism A [i.e., the properly disciplined capitalism the pope endorses] exists only in textbooks." I privately told the dean, a Latin American Jesuit, that if he really believed that, he had no business running a faculty of social science.) But the text of *Centesimus Annus* itself is plain: the authoritative teaching of the Catholic Church is that a properly regulated market, disciplined by politics, law, and culture, is best for poor people. It works. And it gives the poor an "option" to exercise their freedom as economic actors that is available in no other system.

CULTURE WARS

It is not possible to understand man on the basis of economics alone, nor to define him simply on the basis of class membership. Man is understood in a more complete way when he is situated within the sphere of culture through his language, history, and the position he takes toward the fundamental events of life, such as birth, love, work, and death. At the heart of every culture lies the attitude man takes to the greatest mystery: the mystery of God. Different cultures are basically different ways of facing the question of the meaning of personal existence. When this question is eliminated, the cultural and moral life of nations is corrupted.

—CENTESIMUS ANNUS, 24

John Paul II is rather more concerned about the "culture" leg of the politics-economics-culture triad than about the argument between market economists and those still defending state-centered schemes of development. The latter debate has been settled. The real issue is the ability of a culture to provide the market with the moral framework it needs to serve the cause of integral human development.

Once again, "1989" is on the pope's mind. Can the new democracies develop societies that provide for the free exercise of human creativity in the workplace, in politics, and in the many fields of culture without becoming libertine in their public moral life? Will "consumerism"—that is, consumption as an ideology, not as a natural part of what dissidents used to call a "normal society"—replace Marxism-Leninism as the new form of bondage east of the Elbe River?

The pope is not persuaded by libertarian arguments. "Of itself," he writes, "the economic system does not possess criteria for correctly distinguishing new and higher forms of satisfying human needs from artificial new needs which hinder the formation of a mature personality." And so the market cannot be left on its own. "A great deal of educational and cultural work is urgently needed," so that the market's remarkable capacity to generate wealth is bent toward ends congruent with "the truth about man"—which is not, John Paul continually urges, an economic truth only (or even primarily).

The pope seems convinced that consumerism-the-ideology

is to be blamed, not on the market system, but on the moral-cultural system's failures to discipline the market:

> These criticisms [of consumerism in its hedonistic form] are directed not so much against an economic system as against an ethical and cultural system. . . . If economic life is absolutized, if the production and consumption of goods become the center of social life and society's only value . . . the reason is to be found not so much in the economic system itself as in the fact that the entire socio-cultural system, by ignoring the ethical and religious dimension, has been weakened, and ends by limiting itself to the production of goods and services alone.

Centesimus Annus is by no means a dreary exercise in papal scolding. John Paul II knows that the things of this world are important, and that material goods can enhance man's capacity for living a freedom worthy of one made in the image and likeness of God. "It is not wrong to want to live better," according to the pope. "What is wrong is a style of life which is presumed to be better when it is directed toward 'having' rather than 'being,' and which wants to have more, not in order to be more but in order to spend life in enjoyment as an end in itself."

So what is to be done? John Paul II is highly critical of the excesses of the welfare state, which he styles the "social assistance state." Here, the pope argues, is another abuse of human freedom: "By intervening directly and depriving society of its responsibility, the Social Assistance State leads to a loss of human energies and an inordinate increase of public agencies, which are dominated more by bureaucratic ways of thinking than by concern for serving their clients, and which are accompanied by an enormous increase in spending."

Reconstructing Civil Society

John Paul's preference, which is an expression of the classic Catholic social-ethical principle of "subsidiarity," is for what, in the American context, would be called "mediating structures": "Needs are best understood and satisfied by people who are closest to [the poor, the weak, the stricken] and who act as neighbors to those in need." Such mediating structures—religious institutions, voluntary organizations, unions, business associations, neighborhood groups, service organizations, and the like—are the backbone of what Václav Havel and others in Central and Eastern Europe have called "civil society." And the reconstruction of civil society is the first order of business in establishing the foundations of democracy. This is a message that could well be taken to heart in the West, too.

In sum, what is needed is a public moral culture that encourages "lifestyles in which the quest for truth, beauty, goodness, and communion with others for the sake of common growth are the factors which determine consumer choices, savings, and investments." We do not live in hermetically sealed containers labeled "economic life," "politics," and "lifestyle." John Paul insists that it is all of a piece. There is only one human universe, and it is an inescapably moral universe in which questions of "ought" emerge at every juncture. As the pope puts it, "Even the decision to invest in one place rather than another, in one productive sector rather than another, is always a moral and cultural choice."

And as with economics, so with politics. I have stressed here the importance of "1989" in the pope's historical vision. But by "1989" the pope means a set of events fraught with meaning for the West as well as for the East. John Paul II has vigorously positioned the Church on the side of the democratic revolution throughout the world, not because he is a geopolitician, but because he is a moral teacher and a pastor. The Church, he insists, "has no models to present." But, as an expression of its fundamental concern for "the truth about man," the Church "values the democratic system inasmuch as it ensures the participation of citizens in making political choices, guarantees to the governed the possibility of both electing and holding accountable those who govern them, and of replacing them through peaceful means when appropriate."

Democracy and the Ultimate Truth

John Paul II is almost Lincolnian in wondering whether nations "so conceived and so dedicated can long endure," particularly given the attitude toward the relation between rights and obligations, and between rights and the truth, that is common among Western cultural elites today. It is not as Cassandra but as a friend of democracy that John Paul II lays down this challenge:

> Nowadays there is a tendency to claim that agnosticism and skeptical relativism are the philosophy and the basic attitude which correspond to democratic forms of political life. Those who are convinced that they know the truth and firmly adhere to it are considered unreliable from a democratic point of view, since they do not accept that truth is determined by the majority, or that it is subject to variation according to different political trends. It must be observed in this regard that if there is no ultimate truth to guide and direct political activity, then ideas and convictions can easily be manipulated for reasons of power. As history demonstrates, a democracy without values easily turns into open or thinly disguised totalitarianism.

And yet, the pope continues, "the Church respects the legitimate autonomy of the democratic order," and the Church "is not entitled to express preferences for this or that institutional or constitutional solution." Rather, the Church is the Church, and thus "her contribution to the political order is precisely her vision of the dignity of the person revealed in all its fullness in the mystery of the Incarnate Word."

Centesimus Annus is an extraordinary statement of faith:

faith in freedom; faith in man's capacity to order his public life properly; above all, faith in God, who created man with intelligence and free will. It may well be the greatest of the social encyclicals, given the breadth of the issues it addresses, the depth at which questions are probed, and the empirical sensitivity John Paul II shows to the "signs of the times" as they illuminate freedom's cause today. (It is also, despite the occasional heavy patch, the most reader-friendly of John Paul's major letters.) With *Centesimus Annus*, the "Pope of Freedom" has not only marked the centenary of a great tradition. He has brilliantly scouted the terrain for the next hundred years of humanity's struggle to embody in public life the truth that makes us free.

PART ONE

The Encyclical

'A Civilization of Solidarity and Love': An Invitation to *Centesimus Annus*

JOHN PAUL II

At his general audience on May 1, 1991, Pope John Paul II spoke about his new encyclical letter. The following translation of his remarks appeared in the May 6, 1991, English weekly edition of the Vatican newspaper "L'Osservatore Romano" under the title "Confronting the Challenges of Our Time."

1 The hundredth anniversary of the publication of the encyclical *Rerum Novarum* occurs during the month of May this year. As you know I have decided to dedicate a new encyclical . . . for the celebration of this anniversary to indicate, while always drawing on the Tradition and life of the Church, some directions and perspectives which correspond to the increasingly serious social questions which occur in our time. The Church does not look to the past in order to escape the challenges of the present, but to acquire new vigor and new confidence for the activity which must continue among people today, on the basis of firm values and meditation on what the Holy Spirit has done and continues to do in her. The Church confronts the challenges of our time, so different from

that of Leo XIII, but does so in the same spirit: she does so according to *the spirit of God*, whom my Predecessor obeyed by responding to the hopes and expectations of *his* time. I am seeking to do the same in regard to the hopes and expectations of the present.

2 One event seems to dominate the difficult period in which we are living: the conclusion of a cycle in the history of Europe and the world.

The Marxist system has failed and precisely for the very reasons which *Rerum Novarum* had already acutely and almost prophetically indicated. In this failure of an ideological and economic power which seemed destined to prevail over and even to root out the religious sense in human consciences, the Church sees—beyond all sociological and political factors— the intervention of God's Providence, which alone guides and governs history.

The liberation of so many peoples, of distinguished Churches and of individual persons, should not, however, be transformed into an inappropriate sense of satisfaction or unjustified triumphalism.

That system has, at least in part, been overcome; but in various areas of the world the most extreme poverty continues to prevail, entire populations are deprived of the most elementary rights and lack the necessary means to satisfy basic human needs; in the wealthiest countries one frequently observes a sort of existential confusion, an inability to live and to experience properly the meaning of life, even though surrounded by an abundance of material possessions. A sense of alienation and loss of their own humanity has made people feel reduced to the role of cogs in the machinery of production and consumption, and they find no way to affirm their own dignity as persons made in the image and likeness of God.

Yes, a system is finished; but the problems and situations of injustice and human suffering on which it fed have not, unfortunately, been overcome. It has failed to provide a satisfactory answer, but the question to which that answer had been given continues to remain current and urgent.

With the new encyclical the Church not only presents this question to the whole of humanity, but she also proposes adequate solutions. This means a renewed question about social justice, about solidarity among working people, about the dignity of the human person; it means not to be resigned to exploitation and poverty, never to abandon the transcendent dimension of the person, who wants to and who must place his own work at the heart of building society.

3 The social doctrine of the Church has always recognized the individual's right to private ownership of the means of production and has seen in this right a defense of freedom against every possible oppression. Furthermore, the division of property into the hands of many entails that each person must count on the cooperation of others to satisfy his needs, while the indispensable social exchange must be regulated by contracts in which the free will of one encounters that of another. In contrast to the overbureaucratic and centralized command economy, the free and socially inspired economy presupposes truly free subjects who assume precise responsibilities upon themselves, loyally respect their duties to their co-workers, and constantly take the common good into account.

It is right, therefore, to recognize the ethical value of the free market and of entrepreneurial activity within it, of the ability to "arrange the meeting" between consumer needs and the adequate resources to meet them by free bargaining. On this point Leo XIII, in opposition to collectivist theories, vindicated the rights of individual initiative in the context of service required to be given to the community.

4 The Catholic Church, however, has always refused and today continues to refuse to make the market the supreme rule, almost the model, or the summation, of social life. There is *something that is due to the human person because he is a person*, by reason of his dignity and his likeness to God, independently of his presence or not in the market, of what he possesses and therefore can sell, and of the means to buy what he needs. This something must never be disregarded, but rather demands *respect* and *solidarity*, the social expression of love which is the only attitude appropriate to the human person. There are human needs that are not accessible to the market, due to natural and social impediments, but which must be equally satisfied.

It is, in fact, the duty of the national and international community to answer these needs, either by giving direct assistance when, for example, an obstacle is insuperable, or by opening the way to proper access to the market, to the world of production and consumption, when that is possible.

Economic freedom is an aspect of *human freedom* which cannot be separated from its other aspects and which must contribute to the full realization of people in order to construct an authentic human community.

5 Without a doubt, along with individual ownership, one must affirm *the universal purpose of the world's resources*. The owner of these resources must always remember their purpose and the fact that, while they guarantee his liberty, they also serve to defend and develop the freedom of others. When, on the other hand, he removes them from his complementary and co-essential function, he consequently removes them from the common good, betraying the purpose for which they were entrusted to him. No free economy can function for long and respond to the conditions of a life more worthy of the human person, unless it is framed in solid legal and political structures, and above all, unless it is supported and "enlivened" by a strong ethical and religious conscience.

This outline, ideal and real at the same time, is rooted in

human nature itself. Man, in fact, is a being who "can fully discover his true self only in a sincere giving of himself" (*Gaudium et Spes*, n. 24). He is a unique and unrepeatable subject who can never be absorbed into an undifferentiated human mass, and who truly fulfills his destiny when he is able to transcend his limited individual interests and to join himself to other human beings with many ties. This is the way the family is born; this is the way society is born.

Work, too, by its essential nature, promotes the autonomy of the person and the necessity of being joined with the work of others. Man works together with others, and through his work he enters into relationship with them: a relationship which can be one of opposition, competition, or oppression, but also one of co-operation and membership in a community of solidarity.

Moreover, the human person does not work only for himself, but also for others, beginning with his own family and including the local community, the nation, and all of humanity. This is the reality which work must serve: the free and fruitful gift of self is expressed even through work. By confirming the close connection between private property and the universal purpose of the earth's resources, the social doctrine of the Church is merely putting economic activity in the loftiest and broadest context of the general vocation of the human person.

6 History has always known new attempts to construct a better and more just society, one marked by unity, understanding, and solidarity. Many of these attempts have failed, while others were directed against the human person himself.

Human nature, which is ordered toward social existence, also seems to reveal signs of division, dishonesty, and hatred. But this is why God, the Father of all, has sent his only Son, Jesus Christ, into the world, in order to overcome these constantly threatening dangers and to change the heart and mind of man by the gift of his grace. . . .

A great commitment on the political, economic, social, and cultural level is necessary to build a society that is more just and worthy of the human person. But this is not enough! A decisive commitment must be made to the very heart of man, to the intimacy of his conscience, where he makes his personal decisions. Only on this level can the human person effect a true, deep, and positive change in himself, and that is the undeniable premise of contributing to change and the improvement of all society.

Let us pray to the Mother of God and our Mother in this month dedicated to her, that she will support our personal efforts and our joint commitment and will thus help us to build more just and fraternal structures in the world for a new civilization—a civilization of solidarity and love.

Centesimus Annus

John Paul II

The following condensation of "Centesimus Annus" ("The Hundredth Year"), like the full text, is divided into six chapters comprising sixty-two numbered paragraphs or short sections. This condensation appeared in "First Things" (August–September 1991) and is used by permission. The accompanying editors' note explains that the words in brackets were added for continuity in the condensed text.

1. The Centenary of the Encyclical *Rerum Novarum* ["New Things"] by my predecessor Leo XIII is of great importance for the present history of the Church and for my own Pontificate. I wish to satisfy the debt of gratitude that the whole Church owes to this great Pope and his "immortal document." I also mean to show that *the vital energies* rising from that root have not been spent with the passing of the years, but rather *have increased even more*.

2. [This occasion] honors also those Encyclicals and other documents of my Predecessors that have helped to make *Rerum Novarum* live in history, thus constituting what would come to be called the Church's "social doctrine," "social teaching," or even "social magisterium."

3. I propose a "rereading" of Pope Leo's Encyclical by issuing an invitation to "look back" at the text itself, but also

to "look around" at the "new things" that surround us, very different from the "new things" at the final decade of the last century. Finally, it is an invitation to "look to the future" at a time when we can glimpse the third Millennium of the Christian era, so filled with uncertainties but also with promises. A rereading of this kind confirms *the permanent value of such teaching*, but also manifests *the true meaning of the Church's Tradition*, which, being ever living and vital, builds upon the foundation laid by our fathers in the faith.

The Lord compares the scribe to "a householder who brings out of his treasure what is new and what is old" (Matt. 13:52). The treasure is the Church's Tradition, which contains "what is old" and enables us to interpret the "new things" in the midst of which the life of the Church and the world unfolds. Millions of people, spurred on by the social Magisterium, have sought to make that teaching the inspiration for their involvement in the world. [They] represent a *great movement for the defense of the human person* and the safeguarding of human dignity, [and have] contributed to the building up of a more just society, or at least to the curbing of injustice.

The present Encylical involves the exercise of [the Church's] teaching authority. But pastoral solicitude also prompts me to propose *an analysis of some events of recent history*. Such an analysis is not meant to pass definitive judgments since this does not fall *per se* within the Magisterium's specific domain.

I. Characteristics of *Rerum Novarum*

4. Towards the end of the last century the Church faced a historical process that was reaching a critical point. In politics, the result of these changes was a *new conception of society and of the State*, and consequently *of authority itself*. A traditional society was passing away and another was [emerging]. In economics, a *new form of property* had appeared—capital; and

a *new form of labor*—labor for wages, characterized by high rates of production that lacked due regard for sex, age, or family situation, and was determined solely by efficiency, with a view to increasing profits.

Labor became a commodity freely bought and sold on the market, its price determined by the law of supply and demand, without taking into account the minimum required for the support of the individual and his family. Moreover, the worker was not even sure of being able to sell "his own commodity," continually threatened as he was by unemployment. The result of this transformation was a society "divided into two classes, separated by a deep chasm." At the same time, another conception of property and economic life was beginning to appear in an organized and often violent form, one that implied a new political and social structure.

At the height of this clash, fanned by ideals that were then called "socialist," Pope Leo intervened with a document dealing with the "condition of the workers." [Papal teaching] called attention to the essential bond between human freedom and truth, so that freedom that refused to be bound to the truth would fall into arbitrariness and end up submitting itself to the vilest of passions, to the point of self-destruction. Indeed, what is the origin of all the evils to which *Rerum Novarum* wished to respond if not a kind of freedom that cuts itself off from the truth about man?

5. The "new things" [that the Pope] addressed were anything but positive. The Church was confronted, as was the civil community, by a society that was torn by a conflict all the more harsh and inhumane because it knew no rule or regulation. It was *the conflict between capital and labor*. The Pope's intention was certainly to restore peace, and the reader cannot fail to note his severe condemnation of the class struggle. However, the Pope was very much aware that *peace is built on the foundation of justice*.

The Church has something to say about [such] specific

human situations. She formulates a genuine doctrine, a *corpus* that enables her to analyze social realities, to make judgments about them, and to indicate directions for the just resolution of problems. In Pope Leo's time such a concept of the Church's right and duty was far from being commonly admitted. [His] approach in publishing *Rerum Novarum* gave the Church "citizenship status," as it were, amid the changing realities of public life. Her social doctrine pertains to the Church's evangelizing mission, and is an essential part of the Christian message.

The "new evangelization" which the modern world urgently needs must include *a proclamation of the Church's social doctrine*. This doctrine indicates the right way to respond to the great challenges of today when ideologies are being increasingly discredited. We repeat that there can be *no genuine solution of the "social question" apart from the Gospel*. In the Gospel we find the context for proper moral perspective on the "new things."

6. Pope Leo affirmed the fundamental rights of workers. Indeed, the key to reading the Encyclical is the *dignity of the worker* as such, and [therefore] the *dignity of work*. Work belongs to the vocation of every person; indeed, man expresses and fulfils himself by working. Another important principle is that of the *right to "private property."* Private property is not an absolute value. [There are] necessary complementary principles, such as the *universal destination of the earth's goods*. The type of private property that Leo mainly considers is land ownership. [But the same principles apply] in the face of the changes we are witnessing in systems formerly dominated by collective ownership of the means of production, as well in the face of the increasing instances of poverty or, more precisely, of hindrances to private ownership in many parts of the world.

7. *Rerum Novarum* affirms *other rights* as inalienable and proper to the human person. Prominent among these is the "natural human right" to form private associations. This means above all *the right to establish professional associations* of

employers and workers, or of workers alone, and the establishment of what are commonly called trade unions. The right of association is a natural right of the human being, which therefore precedes his or her incorporation into political society. The Encyclical also affirms the right to the "limitation of working hours," the right to legitimate rest, and the right of children and women to be treated differently with regard to the type and duration of work.

8. The Pope adds *another right* that the worker has as a person, the right to a "just wage." If work *as something personal* belongs to the sphere of the individual's free use of his own abilities and energy, *as something necessary* it is governed by the obligation to ensure "the preservation of life." "It necessarily follows," the Pope concludes, "that every individual has a natural right to procure what is required to live, and the poor can procure that in no other way than by what they can earn through their work." A workman's wages should be sufficient to enable him to support himself, his wife, and his children. The Pope attributed to the "public authority" the "strict duty" of providing properly for the welfare of the workers, because a failure to do so violates justice; indeed, he did not hesitate to speak of "distributive justice."

9. Leo XIII adds another right, namely the right to discharge freely one's religious duties. The general opinion, even in his day, [was] that such questions pertained exclusively to an individual's private life. He affirms the need for Sunday rest so that people [may offer] the worship they owe to Almighty God. [We] see in this statement a springboard for the principle of the right to religious freedom, which was to become the subject of many solemn *International Declarations* as well as of the Second Vatican Council's *Declaration* and of my own repeated teaching.

10. Another aspect is the relationship between the State and its citizens. *Rerum Novarum* criticizes two social and economic systems: socialism and liberalism. "When there is

question of defending the rights of individuals, the defenseless and the poor have a claim to special consideration. The richer class has many ways of shielding itself, and stands less in need of help from the State." [Such] passages [speak today to] the new forms of poverty in the world.

The principle of solidarity, both within each nation and in the international order, is clearly seen to be one of the fundamental principles of the Christian view of social and political organization. Leo uses the term "friendship," [while] Pius XI refers to it as "social charity," and Paul VI speaks of a "civilization of love."

11. Rereading the Encyclical in the light of contemporary realities enables us to appreciate *the Church's constant concern for and dedication to* categories of people who are especially beloved to the Lord Jesus. [There is] the continuity within the Church of the "preferential option for the poor." The Encyclical is thus [about] the poor and the terrible conditions to which the new and often violent process of industrialization had reduced great multitudes of people. Today, in many parts of the world, similar processes of economic, social, and political transformation are creating the same evils.

The State has the duty of ensuring that every sector of social life, not excluding the economic one, contributes to achieving the common good, while respecting the rightful autonomy of each sector. Pope Leo did not expect the State to solve every social problem. On the contrary, he frequently insists on necessary limits to the State's intervention and on its instrumental character, inasmuch as the individual, the family, and society are prior to the State, and inasmuch as the State exists in order to protect their rights and not stifle them. The guiding principle of all the Church's social doctrine is a *correct view of the human person.* God has imprinted his own image and likeness on man (Gen. 1:26).

II. Towards the 'New Things' of Today

12. The prognosis of *Rerum Novarum* has proved to be surprisingly accurate. This is especially confirmed by the events near the end of 1989 and at the beginning of 1990. Pope Leo foresaw the negative consequences of the social order proposed by "socialism," which at that time was still only a social philosophy and not yet a fully structured movement. He correctly judged the danger posed to the masses by the attractive presentation of this simple and radical solution to the "question of the working class."

[He demonstrated] great clarity, first, in perceiving, in all its harshness, the actual condition of the working class; second, in recognizing the evil of a solution [that] was in reality detrimental to the very people whom it was meant to help. The remedy would prove worse than the sickness. By defining socialism as the suppression of private property, Leo arrived at the crux of the problem. His words deserve to be reread: "Were the contentions [of the socialists] carried into effect, the working man himself would be among the first to suffer. They are moreover emphatically unjust, for they would rob the lawful possessor, distort the functions of the State, and create utter confusion in the community." The evils caused by what would later be called "Real Socialism" could not be better expressed.

13. The fundamental error of socialism is anthropological. Socialism considers the individual simply as an element, so that the good of the individual is completely subordinated to the socio-economic mechanism. Socialism maintains that the good of the individual can be realized without reference to his free choice in the face of good or evil. A person who is deprived of something he can call "his own," and of earning a living through his own initiative, comes to depend on the social machine and those who control it.

In the Christian vision, the social nature of man is not completely fulfilled in the State but is realized in various intermediary groups, beginning with the family and including economic, social, political, and cultural groups that stem from human nature itself and have their own autonomy, always with a view to the common good. This "subjectivity" of society, together with the subjectivity of the individual, was canceled out by "Real Socialism."

The first cause of socialism's mistaken concept of the person is atheism. It is by responding to the call of God contained in the being of things that man becomes aware of his transcendent dignity. This response constitutes the apex of his humanity, and no social mechanism or collective subject can substitute for it. Such atheism is also closely connected with the rationalism of the Enlightenment, which views human and social reality in a mechanistic way.

14. From this atheistic source, socialism derives the means of action [that it calls] class struggle. The Church recognizes the positive role of conflict when it takes the form of a "struggle for justice." What is condemned in class struggle is the idea that conflict is not restrained by ethical or juridical considerations or by respect for the dignity of others (and consequently of oneself). Conflict becomes "total war." Marxist class struggle and militarism have the same root, namely, atheism and contempt for the human person, which place the principle of force above that of reason and law.

15. The State's task is to determine the juridical framework within which economic affairs are to be conducted, and thus to safeguard the prerequisites of a free economy, which presumes a certain equality between the parties, such that one party is not so powerful as to reduce the other to subservience. Society and the State assume responsibility for protecting the worker from unemployment. Historically, this happens in two converging ways: either through policies [of] balanced economic growth and full employment, or through unemploy-

ment insurance and retraining that ensures a smooth transfer of workers from crisis sectors to those in expansion.

The society and the State must ensure wage levels adequate for the worker and his family, including a certain amount for savings. Improving workers' training will [make them] more skilled and productive. [Measures are needed to protect] especially the most vulnerable workers—immigrants and those on the margins of society. The role of trade unions in negotiating salaries and working conditions is decisive. Trade unions serve the development of an authentic culture of work and help workers to share in a fully human way in the life of their place of employment. The State must contribute to these goals both directly and indirectly. Indirectly and according to the *principle of subsidiarity*, by creating conditions for the free exercise of economic activity. Directly and according to the *principle of solidarity*, by defending the weakest and ensuring support for the unemployed.

The Church's social teaching had far-reaching influence in the numerous reforms introduced in the areas of social security, pensions, health insurance, and [creating a] framework of greater respect for the rights of workers.

16. *The role of the workers' movement* was important in these reforms. Later, this movement was dominated to a certain extent by the Marxist ideology that *Rerum Novarum* criticized. The reforms were also a result of *an open process by which society organized itself* through instruments of solidarity that sustained economic growth more respectful of the person. We thank God that the Encyclical was not without an echo in human hearts and indeed led to a generous response on the practical level.

17. The Encyclical points to the error [of] an understanding of freedom that detaches it from obedience to the truth, and consequently from the duty to respect the rights of others. This error had extreme consequences in the wars that ravaged Europe and the world between 1914 and 1945. There was no

hesitation to violate sacred human rights, with the extermination of entire peoples and social groups. Here we recall the Jewish people in particular, whose terrible fate has become a symbol of the aberration of which man is capable when he turns against God.

18. Since 1945, there has been in Europe and the world a situation of non-war rather than genuine peace. Half of the continent fell under the domination of a Communist dictatorship, while the other half organized itself in defense against this threat. Many peoples were [contained] within the suffocating boundaries of an empire [that attempted] to destroy their historical memory and the centuries-old roots of their culture. An insane arms race swallowed up the resources needed for development. An ideology, a perversion of authentic philosophy, was called upon to provide doctrinal justification for [this] new war. We must repudiate the idea that the effort to destroy the enemy, confrontation, and war itself are factors of historical progress. [When we do that] the concepts of "total war" and "class struggle" must necessarily be called into question.

19. After World War II, [we saw] the spread of Communist totalitarianism over more than half of Europe and other parts of the world. The war, which should have reestablished freedom and restored the right of nations, [did not] attain these goals. Following the war, we see in some countries an effort to rebuild a democratic society inspired by social justice. Such attempts preserve free-market mechanisms, ensuring, by means of a stable currency and the harmony of social relations, the conditions for economic growth in which people through their own work can build a better future for themselves and their families.

[Other countries] set up systems of "national security" aimed at controlling the whole of society in order to make Marxist infiltration impossible. They run the grave risk of destroying the freedom and values of the person, the very things for whose sake it is necessary to oppose Communism. Another response, practical in nature, is represented by the affluent society or the consumer society. It seeks to defeat Marxism on the level of pure materialism by showing how a free-market society can [better satisfy] material needs. Insofar as [such a society] denies morality, law, culture, and religion, it agrees with Marxism by reducing man to the sphere of economics and the satisfaction of material needs.

20. After "decolonization," many countries gained State sovereignty but find themselves merely at the beginning of the journey toward genuine independence. Decisive sectors of the economy and political life itself are controlled by foreign powers. Also lacking is a class of competent professional people capable of running the State and managing the economy in an honest and just way. Many think that Marxism offers a shortcut for building the nation and the State, [and] thus Marxist-Leninist concepts mingle with militarism and popular traditions in many variants of socialism.

21. After World War II, there arose a more lively sense of human rights [expressed] in *International Documents*. The focal point of this evolution has been the United Nations Organization. While we note this with satisfaction, policies of aid for development have not always been positive. Moreover, the United Nations has not yet established alternatives to war for the resolution of international conflicts. This seems to be the most urgent problem that the international community has yet to resolve.

III. The Year 1989

22. In the course of the 1980s, certain oppressive regimes fell one by one in some countries of Latin America and also of Africa and Asia. A decisive contribution was made by *the Church's commitment to defend and promote human rights*. In

situations [under Communist] ideology, the Church affirmed forcefully that every individual bears the image of God and therefore deserves respect. From this process, new forms of democracy have emerged that offer hope for change in [societies] weighed down by injustices and resentments, and by a heavily damaged economy and serious social conflicts. I thank God for the often heroic witness borne in such circumstances by many Pastors, entire Christian communities, individual members of the faithful, and other people of good will.

23. The decisive factor in the fall of oppressive regimes was the violation of the rights of workers. The crisis of systems claiming to express the dictatorship of the working class began with the great upheaval in Poland in the name of solidarity. On the basis of a hard, lived experience of oppression, it was they who recovered the principles of the Church's social doctrine. The fall of this empire was accomplished almost everywhere by means of peaceful protest, using the weapons of truth and justice. It seemed that the order resulting from the war and sanctioned by the *Yalta Agreements* could only be overturned by war. Instead, it has been overcome by people who [found] effective ways of bearing witness to the truth. This disarmed the adversary, since violence always needs to justify itself through deceit.

24. The second factor in the crisis was the inefficiency of the economic system, which is not simply a technical problem but a consequence of the violation of the human rights to private initiative, to ownership of property, and to freedom in the economic sector. To this must be added the cultural and national dimensions; it is not possible to understand man on the basis of economics alone. Man is understood within the sphere of culture through his language, history, and the position he takes towards the fundamental events of life, such as birth, love, work, and death. At the heart of every culture lies the attitude man takes to the greatest mystery: the mystery of God. The true cause of the new developments was the

spiritual void brought about by atheism. Marxism had promised to uproot the need for God from the human heart, but it is not possible to succeed in this without throwing the heart into turmoil.

25. The events of 1989 are a warning to those who, in the name of political realism, wish to banish law and morality from the political arena. Only by trust in the Lord of history is man able to accomplish the miracle of peace and to discern the often narrow path between the cowardice that gives in to evil and the violence that, under the illusion of fighting evil, only makes it worse. [We can see] that not only is it ethically wrong to disregard human nature, which is made for freedom, but in practice it is impossible to do so.

Moreover, man, who was created for freedom, bears within himself the wound of original sin. Man tends toward good, but he is also capable of evil. He can transcend his immediate interest and still remain bound to it. The social order will be the more stable the more it takes this fact into account and does not place in opposition personal interest and the interests of society as a whole, but rather seeks to bring them into fruitful harmony. Where self-interest is suppressed, it is replaced by a burdensome system of bureaucratic control that dries up the wellsprings of initiative and creativity. [There is no] perfect social organization that makes evil impossible. No political society can ever be confused with the Kingdom of God. God alone can separate the subjects of the Kingdom from the subjects of the Evil One, and this judgment will take place at the end of time. By presuming to anticipate [that] judgment, man puts himself in the place of God and sets himself against the patience of God.

26. The events of 1989 [involved] *an encounter between the Church and the workers' movement.* For about a century, the workers' movement had fallen in part under the dominance of Marxism. The crisis of Marxism does not rid the world of the injustice and oppression that Marxism itself exploited. To

those searching for a new and authentic theory and praxis of liberation, the Church offers her social doctrine, her teaching about the person redeemed in Christ, and her concrete commitment and material assistance in the struggle against marginalization and suffering.

In the recent past, many believers sincerely sought an impossible compromise between Marxism and Christianity. Beyond all that was short-lived in these attempts, circumstances are leading to an authentic theology of integral human liberation. [In this way], the events of 1989 are important also for countries of the Third World.

27. In Europe, many injustices were committed during and prior to the years in which Communism dominated; much hatred and ill will have accumulated. It is hoped that all people will grow in the spirit of peace and forgiveness. Between nations, international structures are needed to arbitrate conflicts, especially in Europe, where nations are united in a bond of common culture and an age-old history. A great effort is needed to rebuild morally and economically the countries that have abandoned Communism.

28. For some countries of Europe, the real post-war period is just beginning. They need the help of Western Europe. They find themselves in [such need] not as a result of free choice or mistakes that were made, but as a consequence of tragic historical events that were violently imposed on them. Assistance, especially from countries of Europe that bear responsibility for that history, represents a debt in justice. It is also in the interest of Europe as a whole.

This must not lead, however, to a slackening of efforts to assist the countries of the Third World. What is called for is a special effort to mobilize resources, which are not lacking in the world, for the purpose of economic growth and common development. Enormous resources can be made available by the disarmament of huge military machines. It is above all necessary to abandon a mentality in which the poor are considered a burden, as irksome intruders trying to consume what others produce. The advancement of the poor constitutes a great opportunity for the moral, cultural, and even economic growth of all humanity.

29. Development is not only a question of raising all peoples to the level currently enjoyed by the richest countries but of building a more decent life [appropriate to] man's vocation from God. The apex of development is the exercise of the right and duty to seek God, to know him and to live in accordance with that knowledge. Total recognition must be given to *the rights of human conscience*, which is bound only to the truth, both natural and revealed. The recognition of these rights is the primary foundation of every authentically free political order. In some countries, religious fundamentalism denies to citizens of [other] faiths the full exercise of their civil and religious rights. No authentic progress is possible without respect for the right to know the truth and live according to that truth.

IV. Private Property and the Universal Destination of Material Goods

30. The natural right to private property, which is fundamental for the autonomy and development of the person, has always been defended by the Church. [But] the possession of material goods is not an absolute right. The "use" of goods, while marked by freedom, is subordinated to their original common destination as well as to the will of Christ.

31. The original source of all that is good and sustains human life is the very act of God, who created [all] and gave the earth to man to have dominion over it by his work and enjoy its fruits (Gen. 1:28). This is *the foundation of the universal destination of the earth's goods*. It is through work that

man, using his intelligence and exercising his freedom, dominates the earth and makes it a fitting home. This is *the origin
of individual property*. Individuals [must] not hinder others
from having their own part of God's gift; indeed, they must
cooperate so that together all can dominate the earth.

At one time, *the natural fruitfulness of the earth* was the
primary factor of wealth. In our time, *the role of human work* is
increasingly the productive factor both of non-material and of
material wealth. Also, more than ever, work is *work with others*
and *work for others*; it is a matter of doing something for
someone else.

32. In our time, another form of ownership is becoming
no less important than land: *the possession of know-how, technology, and skill*. The wealth of the industrialized nations is based
much more on this kind of ownership than on natural resources. A person produces something so that others may use
it after they have paid a just price, mutually agreed upon
through free bargaining. The ability to foresee both the needs
of others and the factors [best fit] to satisfying those needs is
another source of wealth in modern society. In this way, the
role of disciplined and creative *human work* and *initiative and
entrepreneurial ability* become increasingly decisive.

Besides the earth, man's principal resource is *man himself*.
Disciplined work in collaboration with others creates the ever
more extensive *working communities* that transform man's natural and human environments. Important virtues are involved
in this process, such as diligence, industriousness, prudence in
undertaking reasonable risks, reliability and fidelity in interpersonal relationships, as well as courage in carrying out
decisions that are difficult and painful but necessary, both for
the overall working of a business and in meeting possible
setbacks.

33. [There are] risks and problems connected with this
process. Many people do not have the means enabling them
to take their place within a productive system. Thus, if not

actually exploited, they are to a great extent marginalized; economic development takes place over their heads, so to speak. Allured by the dazzle of an opulence beyond their reach, these people crowd the cities of the Third World without the possibility of becoming integrated. Their dignity is not acknowledged, and there are even attempts to eliminate them from history through coercive forms of demographic control.

Many others, while not completely marginalized, live in situations in which the rules of the earliest period of capitalism still flourish. In other cases the land is still the central element in the economic process, but those who cultivate it are excluded from ownership and reduced to a state of quasi-servitude. In these cases, it is still possible to speak of inhuman exploitation. In fact, for the poor, to the lack of material goods has been added a lack of knowledge and training that prevents them from escaping their state of humiliating subjection.

Countries isolating themselves from the world market have suffered stagnation, while the countries that experienced development take part in economic activities at the international level. The chief problem is that of gaining fair access to the international market. [At the same time,] aspects typical of the Third World also appear in developed countries, where [market] transformation devalues skills and expertise, thus requiring continual re-training. Those who fail to keep up with the times can easily be marginalized.

34. It would appear that *the free market* is the most efficient instrument for utilizing resources and effectively responding to needs. But there are many human needs that find no place on the market. It is a strict duty of justice and truth not to allow fundamental human needs to remain unsatisfied. It is also necessary to help needy people acquire expertise, to enter the circle of exchange, and to develop their skills to make the best use of their capacities and resources. Prior to the logic of

a fair exchange of goods, there exists *something that is due to man because he is man*, by reason of his lofty dignity.

35. In [one] sense, it is right to speak of a struggle against an economic system, if that system upholds the absolute predominance of capital, the possession of the means of production and of the land, in contrast to the free and personal nature of human work. The alternative is not the socialist system, which in fact turns out to be State capitalism, but rather *a society of free work, of enterprise, and of participation*.

The Church acknowledges the legitimate *role of profit* as an indication that a business is functioning well. But profitability is not the only indicator of a firm's condition. It is possible for the financial accounts to be in order, and yet for the people—who are the firm's most valuable asset—to be humiliated and their dignity offended. This is morally inadmissible [and] will eventually have negative repercussions on the firm's economic efficiency. The purpose of a business firm is to be a *community of persons* endeavoring to satisfy basic needs at the service of the whole of society.

It is unacceptable to say that the defeat of "Real Socialism" leaves [the present operation of capitalism] as the only model of economic organization. It is necessary to break down barriers and monopolies in the international community. Stronger nations must offer weaker ones opportunities for taking their place in international life, and the latter must learn how to use these opportunites by making the necessary efforts and sacrifices, by ensuring political and economic stability, by the improvement of workers' skills, and [by] the training of competent business leaders conscious of their responsibilities.

Positive efforts along these lines are affected by the unsolved problem of the foreign debt of the poorer countries. The principle that debts must be paid is certainly just. However, it is not right to demand payment at the price of unbearable sacrifices. In such cases it is necessary to find—as in fact is partly happening—ways to lighten, defer, or even cancel the debt.

36. In the more advanced economies, the problem is also one of responding to a *demand for quality*: the quality of goods and services, the quality of the environment, and of life in general. A given culture reveals its understanding of life through the choices it makes in production and consumption. Here *the phenomenon of consumerism* arises. Of itself, an economic system does not possess criteria for correctly distinguishing new and higher forms of satisfying needs from artificial new needs that hinder the formation of a mature personality. *Thus a great deal of educational and cultural work* is urgently needed, including the education of consumers in the responsible use of their power of choice. A striking example of artificial consumption contrary to the health and dignity of the human person is the widespread use of drugs. Drugs, pornography, and other forms of consumerism exploit the frailty of the weak.

It is not wrong to want to live better; what is wrong is a style of life presumed to be better when directed towards "having" rather than "being." Even the decision to invest in one place rather than another, in one productive sector rather than another, is always *a moral and cultural choice*. The decision to invest, that is, to offer people an opportunity to make good use of their own labor, is also determined by an attitude of human sympathy and trust in Providence that reveals the human quality of the person making such decisions.

37. Closely connected to consumerism and equally worrying is *the ecological question*. Desiring to have and to enjoy rather than to be and to grow, man consumes the earth and his own life in an excessive and disordered way. Man thinks that he can make arbitrary use of the earth, as though it did not have its own prior God-given purpose, which man can develop but must not betray. Instead of being a cooperator with God in creation, man sets himself in place of God,

provoking a rebellion on the part of nature, which is more tyrannized than governed by him.

38. Yet more serious is the destruction of the *human environment*. People are rightly worried about the extinction of animal species, but too little effort is made to *safeguard the moral conditions for an authentic "human ecology."* God gave the earth to man, but man too is God's gift to man. Here attention should be given to a "social ecology" of work.

39. The first and fundamental structure for "human ecology" is *the family*, in which man receives his first ideas about truth and goodness and learns what it means to love and be loved, and thus what it means to be a person. But it often happens that people are discouraged from creating the proper conditions for human reproduction and are led to consider their lives as a series of sensations to be experienced rather than as a work to be accomplished.

The result is a lack of freedom that causes a person to reject a commitment to enter into a stable relationship and to bring children into the world, or that leads people to consider children as one of the many "things" that an individual can have or not have, and that compete with other possibilities. The family is indeed sacred. In the face of the so-called culture of death, the family is the heart of the culture of life. Human ingenuity seems directed more towards limiting or destroying the sources of life—including recourse to abortion—than towards defending and opening up the possibilities of life. [I have] denounced systematic anti-childbearing campaigns that, on the basis of a distorted view of the demographic problem, subject people to a new form of oppression.

These criticisms are directed not so much against an economic system as against an ethical and cultural system. The economy is only one aspect of the whole of human activity. If material goods become a society's only value, the reason is to be found not so much in the economic system itself as in the fact that the entire socio-cultural system, by ignoring the ethical and religious dimension, has been weakened.

40. It is the task of the State to preserve common goods that cannot be safeguarded simply by market forces. In the time of primitive capitalism, the State had the duty of defending the basic rights of workers, and so now, with the new capitalism, the State and all of society have the duty of *defending those collective goods* that constitute the framework for the legitimate pursuit of personal goals. There are important human needs that cannot be satisfied by market mechanisms. There are goods that by their very nature cannot and must not be bought or sold. [Forgetting this] carries the risk of an "idolatry" of the market.

41. Marxism affirms that only in a collective society can alienation be eliminated. However, historical experience has sadly demonstrated that collectivism increases alienation, adding to it a lack of basic necessities. Alienation—and the loss of the authentic meaning of life—is a reality in Western societies too. In consumerism people are ensnared in a web of false and superficial gratifications. Alienation is found in work when it is organized so as to ensure maximum profits with no concern for the worker.

The gift [of authentic life] is made possible by the person's "capacity for transcendence." Man cannot give himself to a purely human plan for reality, to an abstract ideal or to a false utopia. A man is alienated if he refuses to transcend himself in self-giving and in the formation of human community oriented toward his final destiny, which is God. A society is alienated if it makes it more difficult to offer this gift of self. Exploitation, at least in the forms analyzed by Karl Marx, has been overcome in Western society. Alienation, however, exists when people use one another, ignoring *obedience to the truth* about God and man, which obedience is the first condition of freedom.

42. Can it perhaps be said that, after the failure of Communism, capitalism is the victorious social system, and that capitalism should be the goal of the countries now making

efforts to rebuild their economy and society? Is this the model that ought to be proposed to the countries of the Third World?

If by "capitalism" is meant an economic system that recognizes the fundamental and positive role of business, the market, private property, and the resulting responsibility for the means of production, as well as free human creativity in the economic sector, then the answer is certainly in the affirmative, [although it is] perhaps more appropriate to speak of a "business economy," "market economy," or simply "free economy." If by "capitalism" is meant a system in which freedom in the economic sector is not circumscribed within a strong juridical framework that places it at the service of human freedom in its totality, and that sees it as a particular aspect of that freedom, the core of which is ethical and religious, then the reply is certainly negative.

Vast multitudes live in conditions of great material and moral poverty. The collapse of Communism removes an obstacle to facing these problems, but it is not enough to bring about their solution. There is a risk that a radical capitalistic ideology could refuse even to consider these problems, blindly entrusting their solution to market forces.

43. The Church offers her social teaching as an *indispensable and ideal orientation* that recognizes the positive value of the market and of enterprise when [they are] oriented towards the common good. In the light of today's "new things" we have reread *the relationship between individual or private property and the universal destination of material wealth*. Man works in order to provide for his family, his community, his nation, and ultimately all humanity. He collaborates in the work of his fellow employees, of suppliers, and in the customers' use of goods in a progressively expanding chain of solidarity. Just as the person fully realizes himself in the free gift of self, so too ownership morally justifies itself in the creation of opportunities and human growth for all.

V. State and Culture

44. *Rerum Novarum* presents the organization of society according to the three powers—legislative, executive, and judicial. It is preferable that each power be balanced by [the] others. This is the "rule of law" in which the law is sovereign and not the arbitrary will of individuals. This concept has been opposed by Marxist-Leninist totalitarianism, which maintains that some people are exempt from error and can therefore exercise absolute power. The root of totalitarianism is the denial of the transcendent dignity of the human person who, as the visible image of the invisible God, is by his very nature the subject of rights that no one may violate.

45. Totalitarianism also involves a rejection of the Church. The State sets itself above all values [and] cannot tolerate the affirmation of an *objective criterion of good and evil* beyond the will of those in power. The State tends to absorb within itself the nation, society, the family, religious groups, and individuals themselves. In defending her own freedom, the Church is also defending the human person, who must obey God rather than men (cf. Acts 5:29).

46. The Church values the democratic system [that] ensures the participation of citizens in making political choices, guarantees to the governed the possibility of electing and holding accountable those who govern and of replacing them through peaceful means when appropriate. Nowadays, there is a tendency to claim that agnosticism and skeptical relativism are the philosophy and attitude that correspond to democratic forms of political life. It must be observed [however] that if there is no ultimate truth to direct political activity, then ideas can easily be manipulated for reasons of power. A democracy without values easily turns into open or thinly disguised totalitarianism.

Christian truth does not claim the right to impose on others

[one] concept of what is true and good. Since it is not an ideology, the Christian faith does not imprison changing socio-political realities in a rigid schema. Human life is realized in history in conditions that are diverse and imperfect. Further, reaffirming the transcendent dignity of the person, the Church's method is always that of respect for freedom. While paying heed to every fragment of truth he encounters [elsewhere], the Christian will not fail to affirm in dialogue with others all that his faith and the correct use of reason have enabled him to understand.

47. Today we are witnessing a predominance of the democratic ideal, together with lively attention to human rights. Those rights [are] the solid foundation of democracy. Among the most important is the right to life, an integral part of which is the right of the child to develop in the mother's womb from the moment of conception. The source and synthesis of [all such rights] is religious freedom, the right to live in conformity with one's transcendent dignity as a person. The Church respects *the legitimate autonomy of the democratic order* and is not entitled to express preferences for this or that institutional or constitutional solution. Her contribution to the political order is her vision of the dignity of the person revealed in all its fullness in the mystery of the Incarnate Word.

48. The market economy cannot be conducted in an institutional, juridical, or political vacuum. The role of the State is to guarantee individual freedom and private property, as well as a stable currency and efficient public services. The State also oversees the exercise of human rights in the economic sector. However, primary responsibility in this area belongs not to the State but to individuals and to the groups and associations that make up society. The State could not directly ensure the right to work for all its citizens unless it controlled every aspect of economic life and restricted the free initiative of individuals. The State has a duty to sustain business activities by creating conditions that will ensure job opportunities.

The State has the right to intervene when monopolies create obstacles to development. In exceptional circumstances the State can also exercise a *substitute function*, when social or business sectors are too weak or just getting under way. Such supplementary interventions must be as brief as possible, so as to avoid removing permanently from society and business the functions that are properly theirs, and so as to avoid enlarging excessively the sphere of State intervention to the detriment of both economic and civil freedom.

In recent years, such intervention has vastly expanded, creating the "Welfare State." Excesses and abuses have provoked very harsh criticisms of the Welfare State, dubbed the "Social Assistance State." Malfunctions in the Social Assistance State result [from] an inadequate understanding of the tasks proper to the State. *The principle of subsidiarity* must be respected: a community of a higher order should not interfere in the internal life of a community of a lower order, depriving the latter of its functions, but rather should support it in case of need and help to coordinate its activity with the activities of the rest of society, always with a view to the common good. Needs are best understood and satisfied by people who are closest to them, and who act as neighbors to those in need.

49. The Church has always been present and active among the needy. Active charity has never ceased to be practiced, and today it is showing a gratifying increase. Special mention must be made of *volunteer work*, which the Church favors and promotes. To overcome today's individualistic mentality we require *a concrete commitment to solidarity and charity*, beginning with the family. It is urgent to promote family policies for [among other tasks] looking after the elderly, so as to avoid distancing them from the family unit and in order to strengthen relations between generations. Apart from the family, other intermediate communities, communities [that function between] the State and the marketplace, exercise primary functions and give life to networks of solidarity.

50. From the open search for truth *the culture of a nation* derives its character. *Evangelization plays a role in the culture of the various nations*, sustaining culture in its progress to truth. When a culture becomes inward-looking and tries to perpetuate obsolete ways by rejecting any exchange with regard to the truth about man, it becomes sterile and is heading for decadence.

51. The first and most important [cultural] task is accomplished within man's heart. The way in which he builds his future depends on the understanding he has of himself and his destiny. It is on this level that *the Church's specific and decisive contribution to true culture* is to be found. The Church renders this service to human society *by preaching the truth* whereby the Son of God has saved mankind and united all people, making them responsible for one another. No one can say that he is not responsible for the well-being of his brother or sister (cf. Gen. 4:9, Luke 10:29–37, Matt. 25:31–46). Concern for one's neighbor is especially important in searching for alternatives to war in resolving international conflicts.

52. On the occasion of the recent tragic war in the Persian Gulf, I [have] repeated the cry: "Never again war!" As in individual States a system of private vendetta and reprisal has given way to the rule of law, so too a similar step is now needed in the international community. Another name for peace is *development*. As there is a collective responsibility for avoiding war, so too there is a collective responsibility for promoting development. This is the [international] culture that is hoped for, one that fosters trust in the human potential of the poor, and in their ability to improve their condition through work. They need to be provided opportunities [through a] *concerted worldwide effort to promote development*, an effort that also involves [surrendering the advantages] of income and power enjoyed by the more developed economies.

VI. Man Is the Way of the Church

53. For a hundred years the Church has expressed her thinking [on] the social question, [but] not in order to recover former privileges or to impose her own vision. Her sole purpose has been *care and responsibility* for man, who has been entrusted to her by Christ himself. The horizon of the Church's wealth of doctrine is man in his concrete reality as sinful and righteous.

54. The human sciences and philosophy are helpful for interpreting *man's central place within society*. However, man's true identity is only fully revealed to him through faith, and it is from faith that the Church's social teaching begins. The Church's *social teaching* is itself a valid *instrument of evangelization*.

55. Christian anthropology is really a chapter of theology, and the Church's social doctrine [as I earlier wrote] "belongs to the field of theology and particularly of moral theology." The theological dimension is needed both for interpreting and for solving present-day problems in society. This is true in contrast to both the "atheistic" solution and to permissive and consumerist solutions. On the eve of the third Millennium the Church continues to be "a sign and safeguard of the transcendence of the human person," walking together with man through history.

56. I wish this teaching to be applied in the countries that, following the collapse of "Real Socialism," are experiencing a serious lack of direction. The Western countries, in turn, run the risk of seeing this collapse as a one-sided victory of their own economic system, and thereby failing to make necessary corrections in that system. Third World countries experience more than ever the tragedy of underdevelopment.

57. The social message of the Gospel [is] not a theory but

a basis and motivation for action. That message will gain credibility from the *witness of actions*. This awareness is also a source of the Church's preferential option for the poor, which is never exclusive or discriminatory toward other groups. This option is not limited to material poverty, [for] there are many other forms of poverty—not only economic but cultural and spiritual. In the West there are forms of poverty experienced by groups that live on the margins, by the elderly and the sick, by the victims of consumerism, by so many refugees and immigrants. In developing countries tragic crises loom on the horizon.

58. Justice will never be attained unless people see in the poor person who is asking for help in order to survive not an annoyance or a burden but an opportunity for showing kindness and a chance for greater enrichment. It is not merely a matter of "giving from one's surplus," but of helping entire peoples that are presently excluded or marginalized to enter into the sphere of economic and human development. Today's "globalization" of the economy can create unusual opportunities for greater prosperity. In order to direct the economy to the common good, increased coordination among the more powerful countries is necessary, with international agencies [to assure that] the interests of the whole human family are equally represented.

59. For the demands of justice to be met, what is needed is *the gift of grace*. Grace in cooperation with human freedom constitutes that mysterious presence of God in history that is Providence.

60. Solving serious national and international problems is not just a matter of economic production or of juridical or social organization, but calls for ethical and religious values. There is hope that the many people who profess no religion will also contribute to providing the necessary ethical foundation. [But] the Christian Churches and world religions will have a preeminent role in preserving peace and in building a society worthy of man.

61. After World War II, the Church put the dignity of the person at the center of her social messages. As she has become more aware of the too many people living in the poverty of the developing countries, she feels obliged to denounce this [marginalization] with absolute frankness, although she knows that her call will not always win favor with everyone.

62. I again give thanks to Almighty God, who has granted his Church the light and strength to accompany humanity on its earthly journey toward its eternal destiny. In the third Millennium, too, the Church will be faithful *in making man's way her own*. It is Christ who made man's way his own, and who guides him, even when he is not aware of it.

Given in Rome, at Saint Peter's, on 1 May, the Memorial of Saint Joseph the Worker, in the year 1991, the thirteenth of my Pontificate.

PART TWO

The Commentaries

1

No 'Third Way'

PETER L. BERGER

G IVEN previous pronouncements on economic matters
emanating from Rome and given what Vatican watchers
had predicted on this one, I expected that I would have to
employ all my diplomatic skills to comment both honestly and
in a way that would leave me on speaking terms with my
Catholic friends. Happily, it turns out that such diplomacy is
not required.

Those who believe in the magisterium of the Roman church
will obviously read any document issued by the pope in a
distinctive way. Those of us who do not share this faith—once
we have overcome some irritation at being addressed in a style
that reminds one forcefully where the verb "to pontificate"
comes from—can read such a document in two ways: as a
source of intellectual or moral insight; or as a politically
significant text. In my view, reading the encyclical in the first
mode will yield moderate results. Reading it as a politically
significant text leads to the conclusion that what has happened
here is a very important breakthrough in Catholic teaching
about the modern world.

Peter L. Berger is director of the Institute for the Study of Economic Culture at Boston University. This commentary appeared in
the June 24, 1991, Special Supplement of *National Review* and is
used by permission.

Inevitably, I suppose, the pope emphasizes the continuity and the sagacity of Catholic social teaching in the century since *Rerum Novarum*, both matters on which an outside observer may have some reservations. I suppose it is also inevitable that the pope oversells the value of this teaching: it is offered to the world as "an *indispensable and ideal orientation*." On this I must respectfully demur. If one forgets the authorship of the document, its analysis of the contemporary situation and its moral judgments certainly seem well informed, eminently reasonable, and sensitive to the moral ambiguities of modern institutions. The arguments made are lucid, the conclusions careful. Here and there one can find passages of considerable force; my favorite is the statement that "different cultures are basically different ways of facing the question of the meaning of personal existence." All the same, there is little here that sheds new light on the economic, political, and social processes of our time, and the moral observations are not new.

Emphatic Approval of the Market

But as a politically relevant statement by the head of the largest single religious organization in the world, *Centesimus Annus* constitutes an enormously important event. Although there are interesting elements in other parts of the encyclical (such as the cautious criticisms of the welfare state in chapter six), the most striking section is chapter five, which mostly deals with questions about the economy. For the first time in the modern history of Catholic social doctrine, there is here an emphatic and elaborated approval of the market economy as the optimal economic arrangement in today's world. I don't know if the events of 1989 in the pope's native Poland have led to this fortunate turn, or whether Michael Novak and his little band of pro-capitalist Catholic intellectuals have finally managed to get through the ideological nonsense promulgated by outfits like Iustitia et Pax, but this encyclical constitutes a very big rebuff to the Catholic left.

Of course, there have been spins on the document suggesting that the pope is equally critical of socialist and capitalist economies, and even that this encyclical supports that favorite mirage of the Catholic left, a "third way" between socialism and capitalism (an idea that this pope had in fact already rejected in a previous encyclical). These interpretations cannot survive a reading of the text.

The pope dislikes the word "capitalism"; he prefers such circumlocutions as "a society of free work, of enterprise, and of participation." But then he understands by "capitalism" an economy in which there is an "absolute predominance of capital," without any social or political constraints. He makes it very clear that this does not describe Western economies today, as he also makes it very clear that his criticisms of the West concern various social and cultural trends within it (such as "consumerism" and disregard of the environment), but *not* its market economy. When one adds up the various safeguards the pope recommends against the unbridled operation of market forces, one arrives at a concept very similar indeed to what was first called a "social market economy" in West Germany—a concept, moreover, that has been widely realized, with whatever attendant failures, in Western democracies.

Human Freedom in the Economic Realm

The encyclical describes the modern "business economy" (another circumlocution) as "human freedom exercised in the economic field." It states that wealth today lies in "knowhow, technology, and skill" rather than in natural resources. It endorses initiative and entrepreneurship, rejects protective "self-reliance" as a strategy for the Third World, says that no "exploitation" in the Marxist sense exists in Western societies today, and says that profit is okay as an economic goal.

Most important, the encyclical unambiguously recognizes the "free market" (its phrase) as the most efficient economic system for producing wealth. It also insists that there continue to be terrible economic problems in the poorer countries, but it understands that these problems are caused not by the famous *dependencia* but, on the contrary, by these countries' inadequate integration into the wealth-producing world economy. The encyclical also criticizes the persisting "alienations," in a cultural and spiritual sense, in the rich countries—as do, of course, many of the most enthusiastic proponents of capitalism.

I doubt if this encyclical will induce Milton Friedman to seek Catholic baptism. But it should give Catholics with sane views about economics a much needed morale booster when they have to deal with the *gauchisme* that is still entrenched both in Catholic academia and in the Catholic bureaucracy in this country.

2

The Free Economy and the Free Man

ROCCO BUTTIGLIONE

ONE of the many merits of *Centesimus Annus* is that it has fostered a much needed step forward in the dialogue between the Catholic Church and the American spirit. This step forward is the consequence of carefully drawn distinctions that make some of the usual misunderstandings of the Holy Father's intentions difficult or impossible, and that compel those willing to criticize the Church's social doctrine to come to grips with the encyclical's content rather than battling over words whose meaning and emotional charge often differ on this or that side of the Atlantic, in the northern or the southern hemisphere.

One of these often misunderstood words is "capitalism." In the United States, "capitalism" is a thoroughly positive and respectable word. It implies free enterprise, free initiative, the right to work out one's destiny through one's own efforts. In short, it is a bastion of American liberty.

Rocco Buttiglione is a professor at the International Academy of Philosophy in Liechtenstein. He has written extensively on Catholic social thought and on the life and thought of Pope John Paul II, with whom he has been a philosophical collaborator for many years. This essay appeared in the July-August 1991 issue of *Crisis* and is used by permission.

In Europe, as a rule, we have a different perception. Here "capitalism" implies the exploitation of the masses through an elite of tycoons who dispose of the natural and historical resources of the land to suit themselves and who reduce to poverty large masses of peasants and artisans.

In Latin America the meaning is even darker: there, at least among the intellectuals and a large section of the masses, *capitalism* is simply synonymous with social injustice.

A detailed analysis would be needed to show how one word can resound with such different, even contradictory meanings. In the Anglo-Saxon countries, the free-market economy grew organically. On the European continent, however, the Industrial Revolution was often the result of the activity of small groups, organized and led by bankers rather than by industrial entrepreneurs, and enjoying the decisive support of the state. This meant that "capitalism" was, from the beginning, a *monopoly* capitalism. Even worse was the situation in many Third World countries, where control over all the country's resources was concentrated in the hands of foreign companies and corrupted local power elites.

Shall we speak, then, of different models of capitalism? In part, the formal rules of the system were (and are) the same on all these continents. But the concentration of real power in the hands of a privileged group causes the rules to produce different effects. (In Italy, for instance, only in recent years has a large class of small entrepreneurs developed, resulting in the social acceptance of freedom of enterprise and in a growing legitimation of the market.) It is always possible that power groups will try to close the market, to make it impossible for other persons to acquire the means necessary to enter it. Whether we say that monopoly capitalism really deserves the name capitalism or is a form of badly concealed socialism (as perhaps Michael Novak would say) is not really important. What is important is that we share the same positive judgment on "capitalism" in the one sense and the same negative judgment on "capitalism" in the other sense.

The Market as Social Institution

This leads to a second, equally important point. The market is not a natural state of affairs; it is a social institution. As such, it must be created and it must be defended; it may be enlarged and it may be restricted.

For the market to work, for people to be able to buy and sell in the marketplace, certain conditions are necessary. Some of these are legal and objective. For example, we need laws defending the freedom of individuals and their property, and we need a law of contracts. It is impossible to buy and sell if somebody can take what he wants by force. We also need information about the kinds of commodities in demand, and we need the educational and technical skills to produce these commodities. Those who will take the responsibility of production need a minimum of capital so that they can expose their good ideas to an intelligent and active banker who can provide them with the further capital they need. And we need efficient communications and transportation systems to take our commodities to market.

In some countries these market prerequisites are widely available; in others only a small minority of persons has access to them, while the great majority has none. Here the market does not exist, or at least is severely restricted. Large masses have no choice but to accept whatever is offered them by those who have a monopoly of access to the market. Under such circumstances, something just short of a social revolution is required to create a market: a peaceful revolution of freedom.

A Duty of Solidarity

We reach here a third important point. Even in countries where the market works, many persons remain out of it because of natural and social handicaps. It is a moral duty of solidarity to supply these persons with the material help needed to rehabilitate them, if possible, or otherwise to preserve their life and their human dignity.

This duty does not fall solely upon the state, however. *Centesimus Annus* defends the necessity of welfare politics but warns against the deviations and the bureaucratization of the welfare state. The state should rather, insofar as possible, enhance the activity of society, allocating resources to help families and other social institutions meet social needs. Money channeled through such agencies is as a rule more effective than money channeled through bureaucratic institutions, and different social groups are thereby encouraged to meet social needs by satisfying their social responsibilities. The expansion of large, bureaucratic state agencies, whose tendency to expand does not necessarily correspond to the needs of those whom they serve, is to be restricted.

The Centrality of Culture

A fourth point strongly stressed in the encyclical is the connection between the market and culture. The market is a social institution that needs to be constituted and enhanced through a corresponding institutional framework; it cannot function alone. The market has legal, cultural, and social presuppositions, and it enters into a necessary alliance with various cultural and philosophical positions. In our societies there is a certain alliance between markets and libertinism. This alliance is called in the encyclical "consumerism": market values are the only values that are socially considered, and everything is considered as a commodity, even human dignity, truth, culture, religion, the human body, sex, and other things that by their very essence are not and may not become merchandise.

In criticizing consumerism, the encyclical makes it clear that this connection between the market and libertinism is not essential. It does not arise necessarily out of the nature of the market; it is rather a consequence of a certain historical development. This alliance can, therefore, be replaced by another one: between free markets and an adequate philosophy of man.

The encyclical even goes so far as to suggest that the alliance between the market and libertinism cannot, in the long run, work. Free-market society needs not only consumers but also responsible persons who are capable of hard work and creative action. This need is not met by libertinism. Strong, responsible, and reliable individuals are not produced by sexual revolution; they are born and educated in morally healthy families. It seems, then, that an alliance with an adequate philosophy of man corresponds more to the true essence of a market economy than does an alliance with libertinism.

Celebrating Entrepreneurship

These considerations lead to a final point, which is the most important: the encyclical's extraordinarily positive evaluation of human freedom in the economic field and the function of the entrepreneur.

The free economy presupposes the free man. To have a market requires two free individuals whose wills meet on the conditions of a contract. In a slave society we cannot have a market economy but must rather have a command economy. This simple fact shows us that there is a certain specific value to a free economy. Our perception of this value grows when we consider that the principal cause of the wealth of nations is human intelligence and human will that sees the needs of other persons, sees the natural resources and human skills that could satisfy those needs, and organizes these resources and skills, taking the risks involved in the enterprise. Very seldom has the role of entrepreneurship as the creative side of human work been so clearly set forth and so highly evaluated as in this encyclical. It is even qualified as a specific human virtue, which of course implies a particular responsibility to the common good.

This corresponds, however, to a general principle that underlies not only this encyclical but also the whole teaching of this pope: Nothing good can be done without freedom, but freedom is not the highest value in itself. Freedom is given to man in order to make possible the free obedience to truth and the free gift of himself in love. Truth and love are the measure of freedom and of the self-realization of freedom, in the field of economics as well as in all others.

From *Crisis* magazine (Box 1005, Notre Dame, IN 46556).

3

'Having' and 'Being': John Paul II as Pastor

KENNETH R. CRAYCRAFT, JR.

I F Pope Leo XIII's *Rerum Novarum* was revolutionary in the history of Catholic thought, Pope John Paul II's *Centesimus Annus* is cataclysmic. For the first time ever, a pope has explicitly endorsed the free market as the "victorious social system" in the world, and as the type of economy that ought to be proposed in all places, especially the Third World. Champions of the morality of a market economy and others who care about the plight of the poor will rightly rejoice that the leader of the largest institutional religious body in the world has given his own moral sanction to the free economy.

As important as this statement is, though, it must not overshadow other passages that are more specifically pastoral, written for the moral instruction not just of Catholics but of all who will listen and heed. Amid the rejoicing about the pope's embrace of the market economy, it is important to note the special moral instruction he issues to those who live in, and enjoy the fruits of, such an economy.

Kenneth R. Craycraft, Jr., a former research associate at the American Enterprise Institute, Washington, D.C., is a Bradley Doctoral Fellow at Boston College. This essay is reprinted by permission from the May 3, 1991, issue of the *Washington Times*.

71

Like his predecessors, John Paul II is eager to avoid embracing any ideologies—any "isms." He speaks of freedom and rights but rejects ideological liberalism, "which views human and social reality in a mechanistic way." Even in his endorsement of capitalism, he would rather use a phrase such as "business economy," "market economy," or "free economy." The pope says at the beginning of the document that his purpose is not to endorse any competing world view but rather to analyze "current events in order to discern the new requirements of evangelization."

As a pastor, the pope issues two important instructions that presuppose the legitimacy of a free economy but warn against making capitalism an ideology.

First, he reiterates a specific definition of freedom that, he fears, has been lost in liberal societies. The pope emphasizes "the essential bond between human freedom and truth." A freedom that refuses to be bound to the idea of a truly good choice "would fall into arbitrariness and end up submitting itself to the vilest of passions, to the point of self-destruction." A notion of freedom "which detaches itself from obedience to truth" becomes self-love carried to the point of contempt for God and neighbor, a "self-love which leads to an unbridled affirmation of self-interest which refuses to be limited by any demand of justice." A proper idea of freedom must recognize that freedom is the end of political and economic life, not the beginning. Authentic freedom, in the thinking of John Paul II, is the result of choosing well; it is not the basis of such a choice.

Second: presupposing the moral legitimacy of the free economy, as such, the pope warns about the temptation to excess and personal greed in a free economy. "It is not wrong to want to live better," he says. "What is wrong is a style of life which is presumed to be better when it is directed toward 'having' rather than 'being,' and which wants to have more, not in order to be more, but in order to spend life in enjoyment as an end in itself."

Of course, popes and bishops have issued similar warnings before, but this time there is a crucial difference. Previous warnings against "having" as the purpose in life have been the rationale for a great reticence about the morality of market economies. Now, however, John Paul II is giving instruction not to *nations* about the type of economy they should have, but to persons who live in the free economy he has already endorsed.

He continues to give instruction on how to be a moral participant in the free economy: "It is . . . necessary to create lifestyles in which the quest for truth, beauty, goodness, and communion with others for the sake of common growth" influences purchasing and investment choices. Importantly, he instructs individuals—not governments—"that even the decision to invest in one place rather than another . . . is always a moral and cultural choice."

Many American Catholics have been concerned that their bishops have moved away from their central roles as pastors and toward a role as political and economic meddlers. Some non-Catholics have used this phenomenon to question the very moral authority of the bishops. *Centesimus Annus* is a remarkable document, then, not just because it gives a ringing endorsement of the free economy, but also because the supreme pontiff of the Catholic Church offers a clear example of the proper role of a bishop: that of pastor and moral guide.

4

Goods in Conflict?

MILTON FRIEDMAN

THIS encyclical letter deserves our attention because it comes from the head of a major institution in the modern world, a pre-eminently multinational institution with members in the hundreds of millions throughout the world, an institution that has great influence on the beliefs and day-to-day activities of these hundreds of millions. It deserves attention not because of its philosophical depth or lack thereof, not because of its wisdom or lack thereof, not because of its teachings, however admirable or the reverse, but because it offers evidence of how the present leadership of that institution is likely to exert its influence in coming years.

From that point of view, the message of this document is clear. Totalitarianism, Communism, "Real Socialism" are utterly rejected as political and economic models. So also is the attempt to find common ground between Marxism and Christianity—epitomized by "liberation theology," though these words do not, I believe, appear in the 114 pages of the encyclical.

While rejecting these models, "the Church has no models

Milton Friedman, a Nobel Laureate in economics, is a senior research fellow at the Hoover Institution, Stanford, California. This commentary appeared in the June 24, 1991, Special Supplement of *National Review* and is used by permission.

to present." "The Church respects *the legitimate autonomy of the democratic order* and is not entitled to express preferences for this or that institutional or constitutional solution"—which, of course, does not keep it from expressing preferences. Like any good political document, the encyclical hedges its bets and has something for almost everyone—except Marxists, Communists, and supporters of abortion.

The many ringing phrases endorsing private property, free markets, even profit will warm the cockles of the classical liberal's heart. The sharp attack on the welfare state and the strong defense of the family will appeal to traditional conservatives. The assertion that "profitability is not the only indicator of a firm's condition" will appeal to the neo-conservatives and other believers in "corporate social responsibility."

But there is also much for left-liberals. The many warm words for trade unions are accompanied by none of the qualifications attached to most other affirmations. The pope refers to "workers and other people of good will," implying that *all* workers are "people of good will"! Apparently not even the Polish Pope is immune to the influence of Marx. Attacks on "the affluent society or the consumer society" and more generally on "consumerism" will appeal to John Kenneth Galbraith and his devotees. The pope strongly endorses a statement in Leo XIII's *Rerum Novarum* that "man should not consider his material possessions as his own, but as common to all." The pope asserts that "there are many human needs which find no place on the market." He assigns to the state an expansive role in "*defending . . . collective goods*," assuring a just wage, controlling the market, and performing numerous other functions. So left-liberals and other egalitarians have no reason to feel abandoned by the pope.

And I have touched on only a few of the issues covered in this remarkably thoughtful, comprehensive, and finely balanced document, which is pervaded with high-minded good intentions on every issue ranging from ecology to human rights to religious freedom to world government.

In keeping with its character as a political document, there is little recognition that various good things may conflict, that good intentions are not enough. There is no discussion of the really hard problems of reconciling conflicts between equally well-intentioned objectives. The noble spirit, the good will that pervade the document offer the perplexed little help in choosing among alternative means for achieving their objectives, with two notable exceptions: first, the utter rejection of "Real Socialism"; second, the strong endorsement of the longstanding "principle of subsidiarity," that "a community of a higher order should not interfere in the internal life of a community of a lower order, depriving the latter of its functions, but rather should support it in case of need and help to coordinate its activity with the activities of the rest of society, always with a view to the common good."

As a non-Catholic classical liberal, I find much to praise and to agree with in this letter addressed to the members of the Catholic faith. My stress on its political character, on the dominance of good will and high motives over substantive content, is not a criticism. For the Church is a political as well as a religious institution, and this is a political document. But I must confess that one high-minded sentiment, passed off as if it were a self-evident proposition, sent shivers down my back: "*Obedience to the truth* about God and man is the first condition of freedom." Whose "truth"? Decided by whom? Echoes of the Spanish Inquisition?

5

A Challenge to the
Human Sciences

MARY ANN GLENDON

I F we think of *Centesimus Annus* merely as the new encyclical
on economic issues, we gloss over one of its most significant aspects—its appreciation of the unity that underlies the
fragmented human sciences. There is an of-course-ness about
Pope John Paul II's assertion that "in order to better incarnate
the one truth about man in different and constantly changing
social, economic, and political contexts, the Church's social
teaching enters into dialogue with the various disciplines
concerned with man." But this forward-looking interdisciplinary approach to social questions is by no means the one that
is taken for granted in most of the world's great research
institutions. The methodology of *Centesimus Annus* in fact
runs counter to, and challenges, deeply entrenched tendencies
toward separation, specialization, and autonomous development of the human sciences of politics, economics, law, theology, history, philosophy, and sociology.

In this "economic" encyclical, John Paul reminds us that
economics—like all the other social sciences—is ultimately
concerned with the human person and with culture. Indeed,

Mary Ann Glendon is a professor of law at Harvard University.

as Richard Neuhaus has pointed out, the bulk of the document discusses economics only to place that aspect of human life in a proper perspective. That perspective (equally applicable to politics, law, and the other disciplines relating to man) is rooted in what the Holy Father calls "a correct view of the human person." It is a point of view that treats each individual as uniquely valuable in himself, yet takes account of our social nature, which finds its expression in the complex networks of groups and associations—familial, juridical, economic, social, political—that compose society.

But that does not exhaust the subject, though many social scientists would be content to end there. Man is not only a doer and a chooser, alone and in association with others. He is also a knower. "Above all," the new encyclical reminds us, "man is a being who seeks the truth and strives to live in that truth, deepening his understandings of it through a dialogue which involves past and future generations."

Today's Faulty Anthropology

Since the events of 1989, if not before, we citizens of the liberal democracies have had little difficulty perceiving the errors about the person inherent in socialist thought, with its subordination of the individual to the group, its denial of the role of free choice in individual and collective moral decision, and its constriction of the sphere of human freedom. Yet if we view our own familiar economic, political, and legal structures through the lens John Paul provides, we can see that they, too, are deeply affected by a faulty anthropology—denying our social nature by treating the individual as radically autonomous, and exalting choice for its own sake without reference to responsibility for its ends. As for truth, it seems that, to the extent that our fragmented human sciences are beginning to find common ground, it is on the killing fields of nihilism, where force is elevated over reason, and truth is said to be unknowable, variable, or entirely subjective.

John Paul is not unaware of the problem: "Nowadays there is a tendency to claim that agnosticism and skeptical relativism are the philosophy and the basic attitude which correspond to the democratic forms of life." He reminds us that those attitudes towards reason and truth, as history shows, lead easily to totalitarianism. If there is no transcendent truth, there is no sure principle for justly ordering social relations. The "force of power takes over, people become means and objects to be exploited, there is no basis for human dignity, and no basis for human rights."

Having made this point, the Holy Father is careful to emphasize that the Christian response is not a religious "fundamentalism that claims the right to impose its concept of what is true or good on others." In a firm reminder that in this world we see as through a glass darkly, he writes, "Christian truth is not of this kind. . . . [It] does not presume to imprison changing sociopolitical realities in a rigid schema, and it recognizes human life is realized in history in conditions that are diverse and imperfect."

Living in Truth

What, then, can it mean to "live in truth" under imperfect conditions in a constantly changing world? In words that challenge every practitioner of the human sciences, the Holy Father responds that it means "paying heed to every fragment of truth" that one's faith and reason have enabled one to gain from one's own "life experience and in the culture of individuals and of nations." It means affirming all this in dialogue with others. It means verifying our heritage of values existentially, testing those values in our own lives, striving to "distinguish the valid elements in the tradition from false and erroneous ones, or from obsolete forms which can usefully be replaced by others more suited to the times."

John Paul's epistemology contrasts sharply with the attitudes toward human reason that are now prevalent among the American knowledge class, attitudes that, in the form of a vulgar relativism, are increasingly pervasive in American popular culture. Among the more worldly of our opinion leaders it is widely held that "reason" is but self-interested calculation in furtherance of one's own "references" or "interests." Many of our academic pundits disdain reason altogether, yet—in a strange loop—are often quite dogmatic about their rigorous skepticism. The degree to which these two attitudes have, in one form or another, penetrated our culture poses a serious threat to our ongoing democratic experiment. For they sap our will and capacity to engage in rational discourse about the ordering of our lives together. In practical terms, both come to the same conclusion: politics is the mere clash of power and interests.

Against these irresponsible and debilitating attitudes, John Paul sets the transformative politics of 1787 and 1989—a politics in which citizens are able to transcend, or even sacrifice, in some measure, what they perceive to be their private interests for the sake of the common good. It is a politics founded on a correct vision of the human person—flawed, to be sure, but capable through reason and dialogue of devising institutions and structures that permit imperfect men and women to work together for their own and the common good. John Paul does not pretend it will be easy to discern the common good in modern pluralistic societies. But he does insist that we have the responsibility of using our rational faculties to the fullest, bringing our beliefs and opinions ever closer to such moral knowledge as is available to human beings.

The charge to economists, lawyers, philosophers, theologians, sociologists, psychologists, and students of politics is thus a weighty one. The challenge of *Centesimus Annus* to the human sciences is to assume responsibility for their part in contributing to the formation of culture, and to do so on the basis of an adequate conception of the human person and with respect for human environments, those social arrangements that either "help or hinder [our] living in accordance with truth." The unity that underlies the Holy Father's interdisciplinary approach is the ongoing process of human knowing—the experiencing, understanding, and judging through which we attempt to discern the operation of divine grace, and to cooperate with it.

6

Reordering the World

J. BRYAN HEHIR

IN 1891 Leo XIII shaped his encyclical *Rerum Novarum* on the theme of "new things"; a hundred years later John Paul II has given us *Centesimus Annus* as we debate the need for a "new world order." One way to read this new encyclical is as the pope's contribution to the "new order" debate. Such a reading is defensible if *Centesimus Annus* is read in the context of John Paul's other major social teachings, *Laborem Exercens* (1981) and *Sollicitudo Rei Socialis* (1987), as well as his 1979 address to the United Nations. Long before the change that has occurred in world politics, the pope had argued that the old order was morally unacceptable and had been developing his conception of reform for the international order. He had articulated his view of a world less controlled by the superpowers, his conception of a united Europe—separated from the "logic of the blocs"—and his conviction that the peoples and the nations of the developing world deserve a different status from the one accorded them by the Cold War.

Now that those fundamental changes have taken place,

J. Bryan Hehir is a professor at the Kennedy Institute of Ethics, Georgetown University, and an advisor to the United States Catholic Conference. This commentary appeared in the June 14, 1991, issue of *Commonweal* and is used by permission.

Centesimus Annus celebrates the change and moves on to an analysis of what the moral order requires within and among states.

When Leo XIII wrote *Rerum Novarum*, his primary concern was to respond to the suffering of workers in the industrializing world, but he also designed the encyclical to complement his larger effort to restore the Church's voice and role to a central place in the public life of the world. The effects of nineteenth-century political, intellectual, and economic life and the stances of his two predecessors (Gregory XVI and Pius IX) had effectively pushed the Church to the margins of public life. A major accomplishment of Leo's papacy was the way in which he began the process—intellectually, socially, and politically—of a creative dialogue between church and world.

The setting for *Centesimus Annus* could hardly be more different. Throughout the world today, the role of faith and religious life is intricately tied to major political, economic, and social developments. The driving currents of change in Eastern Europe, the Middle East, and Latin America cannot be explained without an understanding of the personal and social role of faith. More specifically, the place of the Catholic Church on this wider horizon of religion and politics is dramatically different from the situation that Leo confronted. *Centesimus* is guaranteed a hearing in the academies, the embassies, the factories, and the *favelas* of the world because John Paul is seen as one of the catalysts of the transformed world scene. The chapter of the encyclical called "The Year 1989" constitutes a rare insight by a participant in the ending of the Cold War.

That participant is, however, primarily a pastor and teacher. Hence, the long-term value of the encyclical is the contribution it makes to the social teaching inaugurated by Leo. A significant portion of *Centesimus* is devoted to a rereading of the teachings of Leo, Pius XI, and Pius XII. The developing edge of the teaching in *Centesimus* is exemplified, but not exhausted, by three themes: the role of the market, the teaching on the state, and the evaluation of the use of force.

The Market Economy

In the century of social teaching, no other document has come close to the specificity of analysis offered in *Centesimus* about the role of the "free market" in the economy. At one level the qualified endorsement of the market mechanism is analogous to Pius XII's statements about democracy in the 1940s. There is in *Centesimus* a carefully contained but authentic statement of support in principle for the market economy.

The analysis of the role of the market is two-dimensional. At one level the pope offers a clinical commentary on the empirical assets of the market mechanism ("the most efficient instrument for utilizing resources and effectively responding to needs") and of the capitalist style of economic organization ("which recognizes the fundamental and positive role of business, the market, private property, and the resulting responsibility for the means of production, as well as for human creativity in the economic sector"). The clinical assessment takes the market reality seriously and acknowledges values in it that John Paul's predecessors may have assumed but did not assert.

The second level of the analysis places the empirical fact of the market within a moral framework, and describes three moral limits: (1) many human needs are not met by the workings of the market; (2) there are whole groups of people without the resources to enter the market; and (3) there are goods that "cannot and must not be bought and sold."

The market economy poses a double challenge: how to take advantage of what it does well, and how to supplement its acknowledged limits. John Paul's answer is that the market must be placed in the broader context of state and society. He sees the need for a "juridical framework" within which the market will function, a setting of law and policy that will contain the market and address the human needs it leaves unattended.

But what will be the juridical framework at the international level of the economy? The market mechanism is not only a choice that countries can make; it is almost certainly the framework within which the international economy will function. The decentralized nature of international politics has always made the establishment of such a framework very difficult.

The State

A theory of the role of the state in society runs through *Centesimus*; an entire chapter is devoted to the role of state and culture. The tension in John Paul's treatment of the state is that it both expresses his conviction that the state should be involved "directly and indirectly" in fostering economic activity and in defending "the weakest" participants in the economic sectors, and also reflects his determination to keep the power of the state limited by law and free of totalitarian pretensions. This dialectic is found in previous social encyclicals that espoused an activist state, but one constrained by the principle of subsidiarity.

Centesimus is more detailed on both dimensions. Its brief critique of "the welfare state" is new in papal teaching, and it is useful. It stresses the way in which the state—even in pursuit of desirable social objectives—can become an oppressive bureaucracy, and it emphasizes the role of voluntary associations in delivering social services. This critique is puzzling, however, because the range of activities that Catholic teaching—including this encyclical—requires the state to perform, particularly in defense of the poor, is usually identical with the role "the welfare state" has fulfilled in many industrial democracies. It would not be surprising if critics of these functions try to use this language to limit the state's role in the future.

The Use of Force

A basic theme of this papacy has been to foster non-violent methods of social change and to raise the moral barriers against the use of force between states. The Gulf War made the pope even more determined to pursue this course. He refers to the critique he consistently made during the war, and he uses his commentary on "1989" to argue for the possibility of achieving major social objectives—even in the face of state power—without resort to force.

A detailed assessment of how *Centesimus Annus* fits into the wider philosophy of John Paul II on war would be an article in itself; but one surely comes away from the Gulf debate and this encyclical with a sense that the moral barriers against the use of force are now drawn more tightly by this pope. Where he is moving on this question is not yet clear but bears careful watching.

7

A Tribute to the Polish Workers

GEORGE G. HIGGINS

IT has become almost trite to say that the year 1989, which saw the collapse of Communism in Eastern Europe, was one of the most important turning points in modern history. Pope John Paul II, as a native of Poland, cannot be accused of chauvinism when he reminds the world in *Centesimus Annus* that this historic development "began with the great upheavals which took place in Poland in the name of solidarity." That's a matter of record. And in developing this point, the pope rightly pays special tribute to the working people of Poland. "It was the throngs of working people," he says, "which forswore the ideology which presumed to speak in their name. On the basis of a hard, lived experience of work and of oppression, it was they who recovered and, in a sense, rediscovered the content and principles of the Church's social doctrine."

The working people of Poland richly deserve this accolade from their most illustrious compatriot. But also worthy of special emphasis, as the pope goes on to say, is the fact that the fall of the Communist bloc was "accomplished almost

---

George G. Higgins was an advisor to the U.S. Catholic bishops for many years and now teaches at the Catholic University of America. This commentary is used by permission of Catholic News Service.

everywhere by means of peaceful protest, using only the weapons of truth and justice." It is no exaggeration to say that the "revolution" led by the Polish Solidarity movement was unique in this regard. Again, the record is clear on this point and beyond dispute. While the Communist regime in Poland wantonly and in cold blood killed a substantial number of Polish workers in several Polish cities, the Solidarity movement never fired a shot in revenge. It did not kill a single person in its long struggle for freedom. Of no other revolution in modern times can this be said.

Solidarity's non-violence was not simply a tactic. The movement from top to bottom was determined, as a matter of bedrock morality, to avoid at almost any cost using violence against the "enemy." It also forswore giving way to vengeance in any form. As John Paul II puts it in *Centesimus Annus*: "The protests which led to the collapse of Marxism tenaciously insisted on trying every avenue of negotiation, dialogue, and witness to the truth, appealing to the conscience of the adversary and seeking to reawaken in him a sense of shared human dignity."

John Paul II's assigning to the working people of Poland the credit for initiating the struggle that led to the collapse of Marxism in Eastern Europe, and for doing so without resorting to violence or giving way to vengeance, is corroborated down to the last detail in a carefully researched new book, *The Roots of Solidarity*, by the young American scholar Roman Laba. By happy coincidence, Professor Laba's important study was published by Princeton University Press during the very month that *Centesimus Annus* was released.

In documenting the history of the Solidarity movement, Laba painstakingly challenges the view held by some, not only in Poland but also in the West, that the Polish intelligentsia was the driving force behind Solidarity. Basing his argument on a detailed study of archival records, Laba contends to the contrary that Solidarity, as it came to be known in 1980 following the famous strike in the Gdansk shipyards, emerged directly from the activities of rank-and-file workers along the Baltic Coast in the 1970s, at which time the intelligentsia was not yet in the picture. Like John Paul II, then, Laba insists that it is the workers of Poland who deserve the lion's share of the credit for having brought about the collapse of Communism, at least in Poland. And, of course, had Solidarity not prevailed in Poland, it is unlikely that Communism would have collapsed as quickly as it did in the rest of Eastern Europe.

Professor Laba is particularly eloquent—and, again, in full harmony with John Paul II—in his treatment of Solidarity's unswerving commitment to non-violence:

> Solidarity stands out in comparison with other political movements of the nineteenth and twentieth centuries by virtue of its symbolic disinterest in the enemy. No other characteristic shows as clearly the movement's moral renewal. . . . To hate the enemy, to vilify him, was to risk becoming like him. . . . The lack of aggression, the lack of a symbolic portrayal of the enemy is a remarkable aspect of the Solidarity movement. This apparently was an important part of Solidarity's political strategy. By ignoring its enemy, the party-state, it acted as if it were free rather than locked in a life-and-death struggle.

It is safe to predict, I think, that history will judge that Solidarity's deeply held commitment to non-violence, its forswearing of vengeance of any kind, its openness to negotiation, dialogue, and witness to the truth, and its almost superhuman respect for the dignity even of the "enemy" constitute its most important and most enduring legacy. It is good to have a clear affirmation of this role from the head of the church in this new encyclical.

8

The Voluntary Society and the Moral Order

MICHAEL S. JOYCE

In November 1986 the Catholic bishops of the United States issued *Economic Justice for All*, a pastoral letter on Catholic social teaching and the U.S. economy. Five years in the making, the pastoral was adopted by a vote of 225–9.

The five-bishop drafting committee, and especially its chairman, Archbishop Rembert G. Weakland of Milwaukee, were the objects of a great deal of media attention during the week preceding the final vote. In a public address prior to the opening of the bishops' meeting, Archbishop Weakland decried the American experience of "economic apartheid." To redress this "moral scandal," he said, would require a much expanded role for the state. But, he lamented, opposition to greater state intervention would be formidable. The biggest hurdle to implementation of the needed political reforms, in Weakland's opinion, was the widespread "fear of Communism." "It might well be said," he concluded, "that this fear is what unites us [Americans] more than anything." As for capitalism, "the popular conception that capitalism is essential

Michael S. Joyce is president of the Lynde and Harry Bradley Foundation in Milwaukee, Wisconsin.

for the survival of freedom is a fallacy" (*Milwaukee Journal*, November 10, 1986).

Archbishop Weakland promised that the pastoral letter on the economy would not be ignored, as many felt the bishops' 1983 peace pastoral had been. He noted that the bishops had already appointed an implementation committee with a budget of $500,000. But the archbishop was counting on an even stronger trump card: "I sense that part of the lack of implementation of the peace pastoral was that somehow one didn't have the feeling that the papal pronouncements supported it. I sense that the economic pastoral . . . cannot go away because of the things that Pope John Paul II has said. He won't let us forget it."

In the five years since *Economic Justice for All* was adopted, the pastoral's policy prescriptions have not reframed the debate. The reason, however, was not lack of follow-up by the implementation committee. Like the policy prescriptions of the Communist parties of Central and Eastern Europe, they collapsed of their own weight.

Although much of his analysis was deeply flawed, Archbishop Weakland was right about one thing: the power of "the fear of Communism." He used the phrase as something of a put-down. But in truth, "fear of Communism" is merely another way of describing people's inherent love of liberty. And it is in the wake of the collapse of worldwide Communism, most dramatically in Central and Eastern Europe, and the concurrent reawakening of interest in the free economy that the encyclical *Centesimus Annus* makes its appearance.

John Paul II has indeed not let us forget that he has something important to say on matters of political economy. With clarity and insight he instructs us on how Catholic social teaching should evolve to meet the needs of a world changed, changed utterly. But those who have tried to turn *Centesimus Annus* into a kind of papal footnote to *Economic Justice for All* should read the encyclical again.

Indicting the Welfare State

There is so much in *Centesimus Annus* to admire: the discussions of the "dignity of work and workers," of the relation of "human rights to private initiative, to ownership of property, and to freedom in the economic sector," of the family as the fundamental structure for "human ecology," of the notion of an ordered liberty expressed in what the pope variously refers to as the "new capitalism," the "market economy," and the "free economy." But as one engaged professionally in organized philanthropy and deeply interested in the connections between private initiatives and public policy, I am particularly impressed with the Holy Father's penetrating discussion of limitations of the modern social-assistance state, or, as he puts it, "the so-called welfare state."

John Paul trenchantly observes that socialism "considers the individual person simply as an element . . . so that the good of the individual person is completely subordinated to the functioning of the socioeconomic mechanism." A person, he writes, "who is deprived of something he can call 'his own' and of the possibility of earning a living through his own initiative, comes to depend on the social machine and those who control it; this makes it much more difficult for him to recognize his dignity as a person." The reader is left wondering whether this critique is directed primarily, perhaps exclusively, at the discredited command economies of Central and Eastern Europe.

In chapter five we find the answer, and we find something genuinely new in papal social encyclicals: an explicit indictment of the social-assistance state and the "so-called welfare state" associated with the Western democracies. Invoking the traditional Catholic principles of subsidiarity, John Paul II rejects the social-assistance state. It stifles initiative by directly manipulating people's lives, and the result is a multiplicity of public agencies producing "more bureaucratic ways of thinking" and squandering financial resources.

Encouraging Voluntarism

As an alternative to social-assistance-state dependency, the pope eloquently calls for a renewed spirit of "volunteer work," whose goal is to empower the disadvantaged to lead creative and productive lives through their own effort and initiative. Among other things, the pope argues that this empowerment will involve "the promotion of family policies and social policies" that strengthen family bonds and enable the family to be "a community of work and solidarity."

John Paul's prescription for the ills caused by the growth of the social-assistance state is very much in accord with the tradition of American private philanthropy. For the strength of philanthropic endeavor in the United States has been its encouragement of individual effort toward fulfillment of the common good. Private philanthropy in the American experience has served to promote the spirit of voluntarism, individual initiative, and direct personal responsibility for the promotion of good works.

John Paul recognizes another defining characteristic of the American experience with his endorsement of what Peter Berger and Richard John Neuhaus have termed "mediating structures." In the language of *Centesimus Annus*, these "intermediate communities" strengthen the social fabric, preventing society from becoming an anonymous and impersonal mass. "It is by strengthening these intermediate communities that society becomes more personalized," the pope writes. "The social nature of man is not completely fulfilled in the state," he asserts, citing *Rerum Novarum* and the whole social doctrine of the church. John Paul also stresses the "subjectivity of society," by which he seems to mean that man's social nature is first and foremost realized in various intermediary groups, "beginning with the family and including economic, social, political, and cultural groups which stem from human nature itself and have their own autonomy, always with a view to the common good."

The Moral Dimension

Centesimus Annus reminds us that political economy is much too important to be left exclusively to the economic and political experts. The subject has a vital moral dimension that begs for reflection and discussion. The free economy does not create the ethical bases of good character; it presupposes and uses them, as John Paul II insists throughout the encyclical. A sense of personal obligation, self-control of instincts and passions, respect for human dignity, a sense of honesty and fair play: these are among the virtues, the moral habits that people must have internalized before they can effectively participate in the political and economic life of the modern community. In this, and in his stress on "intermediate communities," John Paul confirms a truth that many of us have been slow to learn despite its seeming obviousness: "It would appear that needs are best understood and satisfied by people who are closest to them and who act as neighbors to those in need."

The moral habits conducive to self-restraint and personal responsibility are the indispensable supports that preserve liberty and that restrain a growing economy from succumbing to corruption and degeneration. The family and other "intermediate communities" are the key institutions for confronting and resisting those temptations. And so *Centesimus Annus* provides a crucial moral framework for understanding, and beginning to address, the grave issues that truly threaten liberty and justice for all: the disintegration of the family; the increasing rate of illegitimate births; the perpetuation of female-headed households living in persistent poverty; and the failure of many to exercise self-restraint and personal responsibility for their lives.

Archbishop Weakland was right: John Paul II won't let us forget. But what he won't let us forget are the truths he so lucidly explores in *Centesimus Annus*.

9

Good News, Better News, Best News

RICHARD D. LAND

THE publication of *Centesimus Annus* is an event of great
historical and theological significance. In the new encyclical, Pope John Paul II does not present the reader with
today's usual "good news/bad news" dichotomy. Instead he
offers up good news, better news, and the best news.

The good news is that the pope clearly acknowledges the
productivity and efficiency of the free-market economic system
and gives it unprecedented papal recommendation as "the
most efficient instrument for utilizing resources and effectively
responding to needs." The better news is that the pope's
endorsement of the free-market system is inextricably inter-
twined with numerous cautions about its present weaknesses
and failures. The endorsement is not unqualified. The best
news is that in an encyclical devoted to economics, the most
important conclusion is that economics has severe intrinsic
limitations and at best can only support a political and cultural
system based on moral and spiritual truth.

Richard D. Land is executive director and treasurer of the Christian
Life Commission of the Southern Baptist Convention. This com-
mentary appeared in the June 24, 1991, Special Supplement of
National Review and is used by permission.

In his stated attempt "to 'look around' at the 'new things' which surround us," the pope takes as his point of departure not only *Rerum Novarum* but also the extraordinary events of the last few years, which culminated in the Revolution of 1989. He sees the breathtakingly rapid collapse of the Soviet Union's Eastern European empire as due not merely to the "inefficiency of the economic system" but to the Communist system's social and spiritual failures as well. His analysis of the crucial role played by the churches in laying the necessary groundwork for that revolutionary upheaval will serve as a needed corrective to the many Western analysts who continue to minimize or ignore the critical part played by people of faith in those extraordinary events.

Writing in the wake of the demise of Communism as a viable economic hope for the future, the pope offers his endorsement of "an economic system which recognizes the fundamental and positive role of business, the market, private property, and the resulting responsibility for the means of production," although he would rather call it a "market economy" or a "free economy" than "capitalism." But he makes it abundantly clear that he cannot support the "unbridled capitalism" that much too often characterized the West in the past, "a system in which freedom in the economic sector is not circumscribed within a strong juridical framework which places it at the service of human freedom . . . the core of which is ethical and religious."

The Truth About Man

Informing and driving the pope's critique of the world's economic and political systems—Marxist, socialist, capitalist, totalitarian—is the question of human nature. Again and again he returns to the theme of humankind's "unique value": being made in God's image confers on human beings an "incomparable dignity" that must never be forgotten.

At the same time, and equally, he emphasizes the flawed nature of humanity in its fallen, sinful state. "The fundamental error of socialism is anthropological in nature," the pope says. He reminds the world that "man, who was created for freedom, bears within himself the wound of original sin, which constantly draws him toward evil and puts him in need of redemption." This great and central truth of human experience "has great hermeneutical value insofar as it helps one to understand human reality."

The Christian view of human nature, which tells us that human beings are spiritual creatures with spiritual capacities as well as spiritual needs and flaws, informs our critique not only of socialism but of capitalism as well. Capitalists are sinful, too, and experience tells us that capitalism will produce great injustices if allowed to operate with no checks and balances from the state (government) and workers (trade unions).

If capitalism is more productive economically and less destructive to the human spirit than Communism, that does not mean it should be gloried in as complete in itself. Economics cannot provide ultimate fulfillment for human beings. Capitalism works because it most accurately understands the productive potential of enlightened self-interest in fallen human nature, but it must be balanced with an understanding that people are not just material beings.

More Than "Having"

The pope has some strong and critical words for the libertarian elements in Western culture, for those who are tempted to see the collapse of Communism as "a one-sided victory of their own economic system" and who fail to see the weaknesses and blind spots in capitalist economics uninformed by moral and spiritual truths. An inadequate capitalist system of this kind, the pope concludes,

seeks to defeat Marxism on the level of pure materialism by
showing how a free-market society can achieve a greater
satisfaction of material human needs than Communism,
while equally excluding spiritual values. In reality . . . this
social model insofar as it denies an autonomous existence
and value to morality, law, culture, and religion . . . agrees
with Marxism, in the sense that it totally reduces man to the
sphere of economics and the satisfaction of material needs.

Attacking the "consumerism" produced by such a mind-set,
the pope condemns an economic ethic that defines the "good
life" merely as "having" more and more material things. He
would emphatically agree with President Bush's assertion that
"we are not the sum of our possessions. They are not the
measure of our lives."

The pope makes it clear that "what is being proposed as an
alternative" to the dehumanizing aspects of an unrestrained
capitalism "is not the socialist system . . . but rather a *society of
free work, of enterprise, and of participation*. Such a society is not
directed against the market, but demands that the market be
appropriately controlled by the forces of society and by the
state, so as to guarantee that the basic needs of the whole
society are satisfied."

In *Centesimus Annus* the pope is not so much criticizing
capitalism as "an economic system" as he is assailing "an
ethical and cultural system" for not informing capitalism and
tempering its excesses. The failure to inform, educate, and
regulate lead to "an 'idolatry' of the market" in which "economic life is absolutized" and "production and consumption
of goods become the center of social life and society's only
value." The pope sums up the important contribution of this
encyclical best himself:

The theological dimension is needed both for interpreting
and solving present-day problems in human society. It is

worth noting that this is true in contrast both to the "atheistic" solution, which deprives man of one of his basic dimensions, namely the spiritual one, and to permissive and consumerist solutions, which under various pretexts seek to convince man that he is free from every law and from God himself, thus imprisoning him within a selfishness which ultimately harms both him and others.

While *Centesimus Annus* is a Roman Catholic document in the official sense, it is also a *catholic* document in the broader sense, addressed "to all men and women of good will." There is a gold mine of material in this encyclical to sustain years of ecumenical dialogue with Protestants and other people of faith. I hope and pray that evangelical Protestants especially will interact vigorously with the important issues raised and the far-reaching conclusions suggested in this historic statement.

10

An Encyclical in Conflict
With Itself?

To conclude that *Centesimus Annus* rejects socialism and
Marxism and endorses a market economy is entirely reasonable. There are a number of explicit statements to that
effect. Sound reasons for rejecting socialism are firmly asserted: Socialism encourages envy of the rich; it reduces
individuals to parts of "the socio-economic mechanism"; it
fails to recognize the person as an "autonomous subject of
moral decision"; it renders individuals wholly dependent on
"the social machine and on those who control it."

In all this, the encyclical clearly repudiates socialism and
develops the tradition of Christian thought articulated by St.
Augustine and St. Thomas Aquinas. But when it turns to the
details of "the social doctrine" that the Church now commends, the encyclical both departs from that tradition and
moves toward what it appears to reject.

What is missing, first of all, is an emphasis on the impossi-
bility of assimilating the earthly city into the heavenly city.

Shirley Robin Letwin is a political theorist and the author of,
among other books, *The Pursuit of Certainty*. This commentary
appeared in the June 24, 1991, Special Supplement of *National
Review* and is used by permission.

Although we are told that "there can be no genuine solution of the 'social question' apart from the Gospel," there is nothing like St. Augustine's ringing denunciation of the Christian who attempts to mold the community in which he lives to some ideal pattern instead of merely trying to safeguard an area within which he can conduct himself as he believes he should. Yet it is by their pursuit of perfect justice that socialists have produced the worst disasters.

What is missing secondly is a sharp distinction between the certainty of a geometrical demonstration and the inescapable uncertainty of the conclusions of practical reasoning. Yet that distinction was emphasized by both St. Augustine and St. Thomas throughout their discussion of human law. They taught that there can be no indisputably good law, that human justice is inextricably mixed with injustice, that all social arrangements are necessarily contingent and disputable, that what is suitable for one time and place may be wholly unsuitable for another.

Instead the encyclical sets out a catalogue of universal prescriptions as if they could secure justice everywhere. It requires that workers should participate in trade unions and in the management of industry, and calls for "a special effort to mobilize resources . . . for the purpose of economic growth and common development." No effort is made to recognize or answer the considerable literature arguing that trade unions and worker participation in management contribute neither to the worker's dignity nor to his economic well-being, and that aid to underdeveloped countries has done far more harm than good.

The spirit in which the encyclical commends private property is strikingly different from that of St. Thomas Aquinas, who stressed that the desirability of private property—which he accepted—could not be deduced from natural law and could be established only by practical reasoning, which meant that it could not be an indisputable truth. And when the encyclical says that "the state has a duty to sustain business activities by . . . stimulating those activities where they are lacking," it is endorsing socialism in its currently fashionable form of corporatism.

For all the denunciations of socialism in *Centesimus Annus*, there is no recognition that what fundamentally distinguishes a socialist society from a free society is the difference between a *universitas* and a *societas* that was spelled out by St. Augustine. The *universitas* treats all social arrangements and individuals as means for achieving a given objective. In a *societas*, the distinctive function of the state is not to pursue any objective but to maintain rules that enable individuals to go about their self-chosen projects in peace. In other words, it lays down the rules of the road; it does not plan itineraries. What makes such a community free is that the social order emerges indirectly from the choices of individuals, shaped by obligatory subscription to procedural rules of law. It is not imposed from above.

Because this is the character of a free society, in order to promote it as an ideal for the whole Christian world, the Church cannot go beyond fairly abstract statements about respect for personhood and the nature of social arrangements that permit such respect to flourish. It can teach Christians to appreciate the possibility and desirability of achieving social order indirectly through the unintended consequences of individual choices, rather than through blueprints for securing "rights." It can explain the folly of prescribing the same practical arrangements for all times and places.

In short, if the Church wishes to repudiate the spirit—and not just the appearance—of socialism, it ought to renounce, rather than celebrate, promulgating a "social doctrine" in the sense of *Rerum Novarum*.

11

A Challenge to the American Catholic Establishment

WILLIAM MCGURN

IN sharp contrast to the faith the U.S. bishops continue to place in their government to redress problems, Pope John Paul places his trust in human creativity nurtured in freedom and cultivated by virtue; hence his primary emphasis on moral climate. If this sounds different from what usually comes out of the Vatican, it's meant to. Popularly debated as an economic treatise, *Centesimus Annus* is really a teaching about human nature and its relation to work and freedom. Accordingly, the encyclical's celebration of capitalism is not an endorsement of a specific system but a recognition that the market's foundation on free associations and contracts between labor and capital best enables man to carry out "his role as a cooperator with God in the work of creation."

You might not have known this if, when the encyclical was released, you had to rely on headlines like the *New York Times*'s "Papal Encyclical Urges Capitalism to Shed Injustices," which

---

William McGurn is Washington bureau chief of *National Review*. This articles is reprinted by permission from the August 1991 issue of *The American Spectator*.

misleads on two counts: it ignores part of the story, and the part it reports is not the part that's news. What is new is a devastating indictment of the welfare state and its depersonalization through programs that breed bureaucracy and dependence. No less new is the pope's straightforward celebration of a capitalism that "recognizes the fundamental and positive role of business, the market, private property, and the resulting responsibility for the means of production as well as free human creativity in the economic system."

To be sure, various popes have recognized the legitimacy of different components of a free market (e.g., *Rerum Novarum*'s unabashed insistence on the legitimacy of private property), and non-Catholics may reasonably be bewildered at the claims and counterclaims advanced within the Catholic social debate. But this is the first time that the different facets of a market system have been presented within an overall structure of freedom that binds these accepted Catholic social principles together.

It is not insignificant that the author is a Pole. The collapse of Communism in Eastern Europe is John Paul's explicit point of departure, and he points to the pivotal role played by the free trade union Solidarity: "On the basis of a hard, lived experience of work and of oppression, it was they who recovered and, in a sense, rediscovered the context and principles of the Church's social doctrine." In contrast to the American Catholic Church, where the clergy has usurped many areas of activism better left to laymen, in Poland the dynamic between Solidarity and the Church is much more in line with the role for the laity promoted in the Second Vatican Council. No surprise, then, that in the United States the main criticism of *Centesimus Annus* has come from the clergy.

Why Socialism Failed

This progression from actual experience to conclusions is itself a dramatic departure, and a welcome one. In previous encyclicals, a tendency toward overabstraction probably accounts for the naïve trust reposed in the state, a trust that ignored the degree to which economic powers given over to a state to assist its citizens might easily be wielded to tyrannize them. Socialism took this error to the extreme, and John Paul clearly points out that the fundamental reason for the practical failure of socialism is not economic but "anthropological": its treatment of man as a cog in a machine and not as an individual created in the image and likeness of God. This failure was not without moral consequences. "For a long time," the pope writes, "the most elementary relationships were distorted, and basic virtues of economic life, such as truthfulness, trustworthiness, and hard work, were denigrated." As any other East European could tell you, the opposite of free competition is not cooperation but collusion.

Not least among the market's strengths is that it orders society so that success depends on consent rather than coercion. That capitalism draws participants into free associations with others to advance the causes of all is what Thomas Aquinas might have called virtue formed by habit. Among liberal Catholic thinkers, the market's virtues are usually reduced to a grudgingly acknowledged technical superiority, but it is hard to read the following section and not think that the pope has gone much further than that:

> A person who produces something other than for his own use generally does so in order that others may use it after they have paid a just price, mutually agreed upon through free bargaining. It is precisely the ability to foresee both the needs of others and the combinations of productive factors most adapted to satisfying those needs that constitutes another important source of wealth in modern society. Besides, many goods cannot be adequately produced through the work of an isolated individual; they require the cooperation of many people in working towards a common goal. Organizing such a productive effort, planning its

duration in time, making sure it corresponds in a positive way to the demands which it must satisfy, and taking the necessary risks—all this too is a source of wealth in today's society.

In many ways the pope's description echoes observations made 150 years ago by Tocqueville, who said that, although America boasted an individualist ethic, the salient feature of daily American life was a spirit of cheerful cooperation and the proliferation of voluntary associations. Born free, capitalist man is everywhere in contract with his neighbor.

No "Third Way"

This is not to say that *Centesimus Annus* has got everything right or even that all its parts fit neatly together. The pope explains the reluctance of earlier popes to go as far as he does by denouncing "early capitalism." At other points he implies that the poverty of the Third World is in some way related to the greed of the industrialized world (it would be interesting to have the pope compare countries that have received huge amounts of Western aid with those that have not). And in a number of instances the pope accepts without discussion dubious propositions about the relationship between, say, the environment and a free economy.

But measured against the encyclical's broader themes these are quibbles. By closing off the exits with an unmistakable critique of socialism and the welfare state (both of which are cited by name), the pope has finally slain the false god of Catholic social teaching: the idea of a "third way" between capitalism and Communism. If Catholic intellectuals are a tad touchy these days, it's because they've just had the rug pulled out from under them.

On a practical level, this change in emphasis will have its most direct consequences in the underdeveloped Catholic world, where—to paraphrase Czech finance minister Václav

Klaus—"third way" rhetoric has led to Third World poverty. In these countries, many if not most of them rich in natural resources and pent-up human talent, John Paul's emphasis on participating in the international economy, coupled with his insistence on a fundamental human right to initiative or enterprise, may leave the old protectionist classes unable to answer this new challenge to their legitimacy. In the Philippines, for example, a finance minister whose efforts to bring down tariffs and exchange controls have been stymied by powerful Philippine business interests can now point to the pope's warnings about the consequences of closing those doors. From Eastern Europe to Africa to Latin America, *Centesimus Annus* can be seen as the spiritual complement to Peruvian economist Hernando de Soto's *The Other Path*.

On an intellectual level, the more interesting developments will be in the United States, where many Catholic institutions and thinkers have invested a great deal of time and effort in questioning the legitimacy of market institutions. The initial reaction in these quarters appeared to be shock. This was followed by an attempt to look for the fine print and assert that what the pope says in *Centesimus Annus* is what the U.S. bishops have been saying all along. The bishops were incensed by Richard John Neuhaus's suggestion in the *Wall Street Journal* that they reexamine their controlling assumptions. "Silly," said Father J. Bryan Hehir, one of the drafters of the bishops' 1986 pastoral letter on the U.S. economy. According to John Carr, secretary for social development and world peace at the United States Catholic Conference, "You do not have to persuade the American bishops about the virtues of the market. These are people who have experienced the strength and efficiency of a market economy."

That may well be, but then again John Kenneth Galbraith has become filthy rich on the strengths and efficiencies of a free market he condemns. More to the point, these people like to cite the pope's qualifying remarks about the market and his insistence that the collapse of Communism in Eastern Europe not be interpreted as a unilateral triumph of capitalism. That's true as far as it goes, but it's important to understand the nature of the pope's qualifications and his understanding of a free economy.

Carr and Hehir like to speak about the market's "efficiency," its value as a "tool," and its undeniable superiority in "allocating resources." They avoid any acknowledgment that the market has an inherent moral worth. The issue thus becomes the *degree* of state intervention rather than the nature. The American bishops, so the logic goes, simply draw the line at acceptable state intervention a little more loosely than the pope. But even a casual reading of *Centesimus Annus* reveals that such restrictions are neither the only nor even the most critical limits John Paul sees on the economy. Rather, the pope speaks of a market bound by a moral culture with many mediating institutions, the most important of which is the family. In short, the cultivation of virtue is essential lest trust in the market become idolatrous.

The Bishops' Priorities

This is not an academic question. Just one week before the pope released *Centesimus Annus*, the United States Catholic Conference put forth its positions on seventy-four legislative issues facing this Congress. With the exception of its support for restrictions on abortion, the list is virtually indistinguishable from the Democratic party platform. And except for its support for increased tax relief for children, charity, and pensioners, almost all of the bishops' priorities call for increased government spending or regulation. How many American Catholics know that among the "top priorities" of their bishops is increased regulation of cable television, $200 million in funding for the Asbestos School Hazard Abatement Act, and support for the Democrats' civil rights bill? So long as the debate is limited to *how much* state intervention we want in the economy, we will have missed the pope's point. The message of *Centesimus Annus* ought not to be confined to Bulgaria.

In fairness to those on the Catholic left, let it be said that the general drift of papal teaching these past few decades (particularly under Paul VI) supported their interpretations; we can hardly expect these same people, by and large blind to the moral underpinnings of a market, to adapt readily to an ethic of freedom. Just as important, many of those on the free-market side of the debate too easily dismissed the Church's teachings about morals because previous popes seems to be saying that cultural decadence, depredation, and rot were an integral part of free societies in general and capitalism in particular. Now, certain libertarian absolutists may not cotton to the pope's insistence that economics isn't everything. But the rest of us capitalists have no problem seeing a free economy as only one facet of a free existence.

Throughout *Centesimus Annus* John Paul takes pains to insist that it should not be read as a political treatise. This is not to say, however, that it is without awesome political implications. The real focus of the encyclical is the human person, stung by original sin but endowed by his Creator with a dignity and intelligence that find their full flowering in an atmosphere of ordered liberty. What a message of hope this is on the eve of the third millennium, not least to a developing world accustomed to World Bank studies and United Nations initiatives that treat people as mouths rather than minds. And how much sweeter this taste of freedom from a pope who has known firsthand the bitterness of its absence.

12

Moral Managerialism

KENNETH MINOGUE

T HE pope is the chief executive officer of the greatest multinational corporation in history. Specializing in moral and theological products, it dominates its market the way IBM dominates computers, and smaller competitors (such as the Episcopalians) often try to offer Catholic-compatible components without losing their own special appeal. The Catholic Church thus has to discharge responsibilities beyond its own boundaries without succumbing to the intellectual overstretch that has caused it trouble in the past. It has wisely sold off its earlier commitments to geocentricity and creationism, but in the new encyclical *Centesimus Annus* the pope is advancing a plan for the entire world on the basis of the religion of only part of that world.

The question about the new encyclical, then, is whether Catholicism is being sold to the world, or the world is taking over Catholicism. In the encyclical *Rerum Novarum* of 1891, which the present document celebrates, the Church had moved with some reluctance into "the social question." The reason for the reluctance is obvious. A church is founded on

Kenneth Minogue is a professor of politics at the London School of Economics. This commentary appeared in the June 24, 1991, Special Supplement of *National Review* and is used by permission.

moral and theological beliefs, and would be wise to avoid committing itself to any particular social and political arrangements. The conventional wisdom of the last hundred years, however, has been that these things cannot be separated. Hating atheistic socialism, therefore, and condemning liberalism as an error, the Church moved into the social market with a form of Christian social doctrine that greatly influenced Continental (but not Anglo-Saxon) politics over the last century.

John Paul II has moved on a long way. Liberalism has enjoyed a modified triumph in that the new encyclical is awash with rights of every kind—rights of workers, of nations, to private property, to conscience, and so on. Usually there is an implicit "but" hooked onto these rights, which would be spelled out in terms of Catholic natural-law doctrine. Nevertheless, the pope has gone along with a great deal of the individualist moral terminology so popular today. His basic message is a form of coercive moralism: "violence and resentment can be overcome by justice" is what *Rerum Novarum* was supposed to have taught. If this opinion really was advanced as a truth rather than an aspiration, we can only say that it is false. The problem is, precisely, that people do not agree on justice, and when each of the parties locked in conflict believes in the justice of its cause, the original problem simply gets worse.

One critic has described the encyclical as "schizoid," and different passages certainly seem to advance opposing doctrines. But insofar as there is a clear doctrine emerging, it may be described as moral managerialism. Other terms to describe this feature of the argument would be rationalism, paternalism, and constructivism. The conflicting and dynamic aspirations of the modern world are to be shaped so that they fit into a single organic scheme for the satisfaction of all human needs. Thus when the pope criticizes consumerism, as well he might, he thinks of it as an external influencing principle from which people must be saved, rather than as a symptom of the sinful tendency to idolatry to be expected from fallen creatures. People are ensnared, he writes, "in a web of false and superficial gratifications rather than *being helped to experience* their personhood in an authentic and concrete way." I have italicized the managerial passive voice that dominates the conception of a world policy for worldly salvation with which we are presented. This is the language of contemporary moralism rather than the theology of Christianity.

"What is called for is a special effort to mobilize resources, which are not lacking in the world as a whole, for the purpose of economic growth and common development, redefining the priorities and hierarchies of values on the basis of which economic and political choices are made." This remarkable passage dramatically illustrates how the spirit of the times hops over the barriers of conflict to dominate all parties, for it is the purest expression of central planning as the solution to big problems. Many have said that in this encyclical the pope comes out in favor of capitalism, even if a somewhat "bridled" capitalism. It is indeed true that profit is recognized as a legitimate economic factor in judging the viability of productive enterprise, but what this Polish pope cannot recognize is that capitalism is inseparable from risk and a certain kind of game-playing. Profit is to entrepreneurs what goals are to footballers, and both activities are essentially competitive. But an economy is not merely competitive; it is also open-ended. Where it will lead we do not know. This encyclical resembles a lot of socialist literature in assuming that the basic problem is management and distribution.

There is thus a failure of match between the new and welcome recognition of the values of a free society on the one hand, and Aristotelian organicism on the other. The reason may well be a significant tension between the Christian religion and the way in which the modern world has developed. Just as umbrella manufacturers prosper best in wet seasons, so religion is the thing for adversity. It is indeed the great thing to console us in circumstances of oppression. While Communist tyranny is an unmistakable evil, capitalist affluence may well be more of a threat to the Church.

13

An Argument About Human Nature

RICHARD JOHN NEUHAUS

"CAN it perhaps be said that, after the failure of Communism, capitalism is the victorious social system, and that capitalism should be the goal of the countries now making efforts to rebuild their economy and society?" John Paul asks the question in *Centesimus Annus*. The answer: If by capitalism is meant the "primitive" and often "ruthless" system criticized by Leo XIII in *Rerum Novarum* a century ago, "the reply is certainly negative." But then this: "If by capitalism is meant an economic system which recognizes the fundamental and positive role of business, the market, private property, and the resulting responsibility for the means of production, as well as free human creativity in the economic sector, then the answer is certainly in the affirmative."

John Paul affirms a new capitalism. But the term he prefers is simply "free economy." Of course socialism is economically disastrous, but what he calls the "evil" of the system imposed by the Communist "empire" is its denial of freedom. Readers will miss the gravamen of this encyclical if they do not

---

Richard John Neuhaus is the editor-in-chief of *First Things*, A Monthly Journal of Religion and Public Life. This essay appeared in the *Wall Street Journal*, May 2, 1991, and is reprinted by permission.

recognize that it is, first and most importantly, an argument about human nature. Capitalism is the economic corollary of the Christian understanding of man's nature and destiny.

The pope says that we can now see how prescient Leo XIII was in his scathing critique of the socialist idea 100 years ago. John Paul underscores, too, *Rerum Novarum*'s vigorous defense of private property as essential to human freedom, dignity, and prosperity. According to the pope's argument, interpretations of Catholic social teaching along socialist or semi-socialist lines, together with the idea that the Church proposes a "third way" between capitalism and socialism, are in serious error.

A Challenge to Conventional Wisdom

Centesimus Annus must surely prompt a careful, and perhaps painful, rethinking of conventional wisdom about Catholic social teaching. It may be, for instance, that the controlling assumptions of the American bishops' 1986 pastoral letter, *Economic Justice for All*, must now be recognized as unrepresentative of the Church's authoritative teaching.

John Paul repeatedly insists that economic growth and the production of wealth are essential to economic justice. Private property must be put to its proper purpose: "Ownership of the means of production . . . is just and legitimate if it serves useful work. It becomes illegitimate, however, when it is not utilized or when it serves to impede the work of others, in an effort to gain a profit which is not the result of the overall expansion of work and the wealth of society."

The free economy in advanced societies is still not free enough, says the pope. It must develop more fully to include labor and management in a free "community of work" and "circle of exchange" in which business is viewed as a "society of persons." At several points he emphasizes the importance of trade unions, insisting, however, that they must be genuinely free associations that are clear about "the impossible compromise between Christianity and Marxism."

The pope writes that Catholic social teaching, from *Rerum Novarum* to the present, "criticizes two social and economic systems: socialism and liberalism." In the European manner, he means by liberalism what in this country is commonly called libertarianism. *Centesimus* is as hard on the libertarians as it is on the socialists. While economics is important indeed, man must never be reduced to the merely economic. To think that the entirety of social life is to be determined by market exchanges is to run "the risk of an 'idolatry' of the market, an idolatry which ignores the existence of goods which by their nature are not and cannot be mere commodities."

Putting Economics in Its Place

While the bulk of the 114 pages of the encyclical is devoted to economics, its import is to deflate the importance of the economic. Economics, politics, culture—these three define the social order, and the greatest of these is culture. At the heart of culture is the spiritual and moral.

Capitalism, if it is to work, cannot be amoral. "Important virtues are involved in this process," the pope writes, "such as diligence, industriousness, prudence in undertaking reasonable risks, reliability and fidelity in interpersonal relationships, as well as courage in carrying out decisions which are difficult and painful but necessary, both for the overall working of a business and in meeting possible setbacks."

The economics of freedom does not assume the practice of unqualified altruism. The pope has no illusions about human nature. "Man, who was created for freedom, bears within himself the wound of original sin which constantly draws him towards evil and puts him in need of redemption." Self-interest is often wrongly perceived, but it cannot be eliminated. An economy that is fit for human nature must take legitimate self-interest into account. "The social order will be all the more stable, the more . . . it does not place in opposition personal interest and the interest of society as a whole, but rather seeks ways to bring them into fruitful harmony. In fact, where self-interest is violently suppressed, it is replaced by a burdensome system of bureaucratic control which dries up the wellsprings of initiative and creativity."

Similarly, profit is not to be despised. "The Church acknowledges the legitimate role of profit as an indication that a business is functioning well." At the same time, "profitability is not the only indicator of a firm's condition." The "most valuable asset" of a company is its people. When they are "humiliated and their dignity offended," this both is "morally impermissible" and "will eventually have negative repercussions on the firm's economic efficiency."

The pope points out that the production of wealth has increasingly less to do with the exploitation of natural resources and more to do with the employment of human resources—with the intelligence, skills, and creativity of people who recognize that individual good and common good are inseparably joined in the expanding solidarity of "the community of work."

The Abuse of Freedom

Despite his respect for the market mechanism, the pope is severely, even harshly critical of much in those advanced societies that do practice economic freedom. No proponent of capitalism should want to deny the justice of his critique, for the problem, John Paul makes abundantly clear, is not with economic freedom but with the abuse of that freedom. The remedies are essentially cultural, political, and, finally, spiritual. He bitingly condemns the "consumerism" that results when "freedom refuses to be bound to the truth and falls into arbitrariness and ends up submitting itself to the vilest of passions, to the point of self-destruction." The practice of abortion, he observes several times, is an alarming indicator of the degradation of human dignity.

Catholics with a stake in protecting anti-capitalist prejudices have claimed that John Paul is faulting capitalism for the social sins that he deplores. That claim flies in the face of the pope's own words: "These criticisms are directed not so much against an economic system as against an ethical and cultural system. . . . If economic life is absolutist, if the production and consumption of goods become the center of social life and society's only values, the reason is not to be found not so much in the economic system itself as in the fact that the entire socio-cultural system, by ignoring the ethical and religious dimension, has been weakened, and ends up by limiting itself to the production of goods and services alone."

In other words, there is only so much that economics can do. The free market cannot produce the virtuous society that the economy itself requires. That is the task of culture and, most particularly, of morality and religion.

As economics is limited, so also is the role of politics. "The State," the pope writes, "has the task of determining the juridical framework within which economic affairs are to be conducted, and thus of safeguarding the prerequisites of a free economy." Thus, for example, monopolies must not be permitted to exclude competition in the market. The free economy cannot be conducted in an "institutional, juridical, or political vacuum." "On the contrary, it presupposes sure guarantees of individual freedom and private property, as well as a stable currency and efficient public services." In a free society, the state is a servant with carefully circumscribed duties.

John Paul is highly critical of the expansive ambitions of government in what he calls the "Welfare State" or the "Social Assistance State." He reluctantly allows that in "exceptional circumstances," mainly in economically undeveloped societies, the state may make "supplementary interventions." But such interventions "must be as brief as possible, so as to avoid removing permanently from society and business systems the functions which are properly theirs, and so as to avoid enlarging excessively the sphere of State intervention to the detriment of both economic and civil freedom."

This insight is based on two principles that run through the encyclical. The first is the principle of priority. The individual, his free associations, and society itself are all prior to the state in both dignity and rights. The second is the principle of subsidiarity: "A community of a higher order should not interfere in the internal life of a community of a lower order, depriving the latter of its functions, but rather should support it in case of need and help to coordinate its activity with the activities of the rest of society, always with a view to the common good."

Challenges to the "New Capitalism"

While *Centesimus* is a ringing affirmation of the free economy, there is nothing in it to justify complacency among the friends of capitalism. Socialism is dead, but "the new capitalism" has hardly met the challenges raised by the pope. He presses three of these with particular urgency.

First, the principle of subsidiarity requires that advanced societies redesign their social policies to return power to "the intermediate groups" of family and voluntary associations. Social policies should be designed and implemented at the levels nearest to those most immediately affected by them.

Second, the pope offers a number of proposals for the more effective inclusion of poor nations in the world economy's "community of work" and "circle of exchange." As the spiritual leader of nearly a billion Christians, most of them poor, the pope necessarily has much to say about poverty. The chief problem of the poor, he contends, is not capitalism but their "marginalization" from capitalism. While acknowledging the ways in which poor nations are responsible for their own plight, John Paul insists that the more developed economies must do much more to address their marginalization.

Third, business leaders are called upon to disenthrall themselves from the illusion that their decisions are morally neutral. What business does either advances or impedes the prospect, nationally and globally, of "a society of free work, of enterprise, and of participation." Each of us is accountable to that common good and, finally, to the judgment of God.

Far from being an uncritical blessing of the market economy, then, the message of *Centesimus Annus* is that the work of "the new capitalism" has hardly begun.

14

The Meaning of
'In God's Image'

JACOB NEUSNER

IN the majesty of its profound vision of humanity, *Centesimus Annus* is a document worthy of the august office of its author. Its power derives from the insistence that theological anthropology inform social policy. Christianity and Judaism view humanity as being "in God's image," using the biblical language "in our image, after our likeness." A coherent account of the social order, such as the magisterium has now set forth for the faithful, then flows from the theological vision of in what way we are "like God."

The pathos of this document is in its limited grasp of large conflict. The pope sees humanity with a smiling face. But the face of humanity is not always smiling. The encyclical's insistence ("war never again") that war never does good and never is just, its explanation of how humanity gains a clear advantage over evil, and its account of the source of human misery—all attest to an awry perception of "in our image, after our likeness."

Jacob Neusner is graduate research professor of religious studies at the University of South Florida, in Tampa. This commentary appeared in the June 24, 1991, Special Supplement of *National Review* and is used by permission.

131

1. "War never again" does not tell us what to do when an Iraq grabs a Kuwait. The explicit condemnation of President Bush's leadership is deplorable.

2. The pope explains what happened in 1989 as "an example of the willingness to negotiate and of the Gospel spirit in the face of an adversary determined not to be bound by moral principles." Maybe so. But if the Communists could have held on to their empire, they would have. If they could have added Western Europe, the gospel spirit would not have stopped their tanks. NATO kept them at bay. The patient, indomitable spirit of the American people, embodied in President Reagan's "evil empire" speech, as much as Christianity, explains the *annus mirabilis*, 1989. We stood firm; they gave way.

3. The pope's account of why the Third and Fourth Worlds wallow in misery expresses his noble theological anthropology. But he does not invoke as reasons for the human degradation of much of Asia, Africa, and Latin America the facts of overpopulation, corrupt politics, and maldistributive economics. If we are in God's image, then I suppose some imagine there cannot be too many of us. But clearly there are. Silence on the matter of family planning reminds us of the unhappy encyclical on birth control, implausible to Catholics, as Father Andrew Greeley has demonstrated, and irrelevant to others. With all my heart I affirm that abortion as post facto birth control is murder. But, along with critics even in the Church, I must regret that the lack of family planning in the Third and Fourth Worlds plays no part in the pope's picture of the distortion of the human image there.

For these reasons I find in the implicit theological anthropology of the encyclical a somewhat limited account of what it means to be humanity "in God's image." The proposed theory of the social order loses its clear focus, I think, because of its astigmatic vision of who we are and what it means to bear God's image as we do. Others, with a different account of humanity in God's image, are then left to cope with conflict and contradiction, forming for themselves a more nuanced, perhaps more complex, anthropology to tell us how to live, yes, in God's image, but also in the tough reality that God has made for us, and of us.

It is time for a theological debate on the social order, and the theologians too—Christian, Judaic, and Muslim alike— bear responsibility for their views of public policy. For it is clear, these days, that the world is listening. The other gods have failed; it is time, now, for God. The intellectual elegance of *Centesimus Annus* has won for theology a solemn hearing. But to speak in God's name, we have still to persuade humanity.

15

The Poverty of the West

GERHART NIEMEYER

G LOBAL politics has slid into a new period that deserves to be called "totalitarianism in reform." We are faced with wholly unprecedented phenomena and problems to which our old generalities and clichés do not apply. A case in point is the tendency of some otherwise serious thinkers to speak of Communist hard-liners as "conservatives" and, when this meets with raised eyebrows, to explain lamely: "It is because they desire to preserve their tradition." As if there could be any such thing as a tradition of Communism! Thus few people have anything of real insight to say in this situation. *Centesimus Annus*, however, has much to say, and it speaks "as one having authority, and not as the scribes."

The encyclical, on principle, endorses our economic system from a point of view that embraces all of human life and human nature. It mentions specifically "the fundamental and positive role of business, the market, private property, and the resulting responsibility for the means of production, as well as free human creativity in the economic sector." Does this approval leave out anything essential? The pope dislikes the

---

Gerhart Niemeyer is an Episcopal canon and an emeritus professor of political science at Notre Dame. This commentary appeared in the June 24, 1991, Special Supplement of *National Review* and is used by permission.

term "capitalism"; he prefers "business economy," "market economy," or "free economy." Who would object? True, some details of the analysis might have been more accurate. Thus the market is not "an instrument"; rather, in the midst of millions of subjective interests seeking relation, it is the sole objective reality that permits comparative valuations and, because it does not depend on any particular human will, serves as a guarantee of individual freedom. Then again, profit is not "legitimate" merely because it is "an indication that a business is functioning well"; it must also be seen as the source of capital required for improvement, growth, innovation.

Along with this praise, however, comes a profound and precise critique of the West. Americans may rejoice because, insofar as this critique demands the creation of certain additional institutions in capitalist societies, we find that we already have them. But the pope's attack on "consumerism" we cannot evade. He defines it as "a style of life which is presumed to be better when it is directed toward 'having' rather than 'being.'" The pope also chastises "the poverty and narrowness of man's outlook" when, regarding nature, he "sets himself up in place of God." We have heard a similar criticism before, from Solzhenitsyn, to which we reacted by closing out from our mind and our memory not only his words but also his person. I believe these criticisms to be true, so I should hope that we will take this recent one seriously.

If I dare to be critical of the encyclical, it is not from a motive of self-defense. The encyclical's critique of the West seems to be more institutional than it should and need to have been. All too often it treats Marxism as "a philosophy," or an attempt to "solve" a serious social problem, "the worker question." Marx certainly was no philosopher (lover of wisdom) but an ideologue, a category he shared with Auguste Comte, Mikhail Bakunin, Georges Sorel, and many more. Common to them all was a Romantic ambition to make a new reality, create a new man, dominate and complete history—in other words, "save" mankind while rejecting God and transcendence. It was such Promethean ambition that Aeschylus described as "no small madness."

Insofar as the ideologues linked their basic will to power with some human grievance, they "exploited" injustice and oppression for their own ulterior motives. Ideologies had become possible in the nineteenth century, because the Enlightenment had destroyed "authentic philosophy" by perverting the concept of reason into that of an exclusively human power tool with unlimited possibilities. To this, Romantic thinking added the Promethean vision.

The West thus suffers not so much from institutional ills as from a crisis of the spirit ("pneumopathology" was Schelling's name for it). The armed ideological movements and regimes of our time are like big festering boils on a diseased body. The boils have burst, finally also in the East. The virus causing the disease, however, persists in the West. Such symbols of philosophical insight as the concepts "being," "nature," "soul," "man," and "transcendence" have utterly gone from the professional literature, academic teaching, and jurisprudence. In their absence we experience disorientation, or "alienation," as the encyclical calls it.

The pope's warning to us not to consider ourselves the global "victor" whose order must be a model to all the world should be heeded, in any case. We must realize that "totalitarianism in reform" is not just "their" problem but ours, too. Most of the Eastern European nations attained freedom without violence. Nor were the workers the ones who everywhere marched in front. From great and long-endured suffering these peoples found the courage to say *No!* to the despotism of untruth.

That means, however, that our relation to these people must not be that of a rich uncle toward a poor country relative. Rather, it is a meeting of one kind of poverty with another. If they lack productive property, as well as capital and managerial skills, our poverty is what the pope calls "the loss of the authentic meaning of life." The meeting must not be one of giving on one side and taking on the other, but rather of mutual giving and taking, different gifts for different needs, and together a great effort to move toward the freedom of truth.

16

Tested by Our Own Ideals

MICHAEL NOVAK

THE encyclical *Centesimus Annus* does what many of us had long hoped some church authority would do: it captures the spirit and essence of the American experiment in political economy. The pope showed an extraordinary grasp of American ideas, achievements, and points of view. His vision of a free economy, within a culture moral and religious to its core, guided and energized by a democratic polity, is American in spirit and definition. Thus Pope John Paul II has brought economic liberty (plus democracy) into Catholic social teaching, just as Vatican II brought in religious liberty. In both cases, these are predominantly American contributions to the church universal.

The big points in this encyclical will surely be covered by other writers in this volume. I'd like to concentrate on a few small points, since it is in its details that this papal letter shows its true brilliance. Just one example: The pope describes the desperate need poor families have of jobs. But instead of declaring a Humphrey-Hawkins "right to work" that the state would have to enforce, he writes: "Primary responsibility [for

Michael Novak holds the George Frederick Jewett Chair in Religion and Public Policy at the American Enterprise Institute. This commentary appeared in the June 24, 1991, Special Supplement of *National Review* and is used by permission.

human rights in the economic sector] belongs not to the state but to individuals and to the various groups and associations which make up society." Then comes a sentence I love: "The state could not directly ensure the right to work for all its citizens unless it controlled every aspect of economic life and restricted the free initiative of individuals." Having experienced the prison fashioned by the Marxist version of "economic rights," the pope pops that notion of rights on its glass chin, and the fragments fall to the floor.

Another detail shines out in the section on drugs, which the pope points to as a sign of "consumerism" at its worst: "These criticisms are directed not so much against an economic system as against an ethical and cultural system." What a neat—and accurate—way of putting it.

Three Systems in Society

Throughout, this philosophically trained pope distinguishes the three separate but related systems of advanced free societies: the political system, the economic system, and the moral-cultural system. To each he gives its due, as he also gives its due to their necessary unity, as checks and balances to one another. (It does not seem hard for a person trained to discuss the Trinity to grasp a concept of three-in-one.)

Further neat distinctions are made, for the first time in a papal document, between human capital and capital based on land, and between nations in the "South" that are poor and those that use human capital to create much wealth despite their lack of natural resources. The pope identifies the chief causes of the wealth of nations—not a Marxist "labor theory of value," but enterprise, innovation, organizing skill, and creativity: "Today the decisive factor increasingly is *man himself*, that is, his knowledge, especially his scientific knowledge, his capacity for interrelated and compact organization, as well as his ability to perceive the needs of others and to satisfy them." The pope's further elaboration of new modern virtues such as enterprise, initiative, creativity, and civic responsibility is also superb.

The Moral/Cultural Agenda

Most important of all, perhaps, is the extended attention given throughout *Centesimus Annus* to the moral and cultural sector of life—how it impinges on the political economy, often inspiring, correcting, and guiding it while imparting to it dynamism and character. A pope who has experienced both Communist and free societies understands instantly the economic differences that moral/cultural factors give rise to. For free societies in the twenty-first century, questions of culture and morals are likely to be near the top of the agenda. Amid rising tides of intellectual relativism and moral sickness, free societies face real problems in developing their human capital and in maintaining against human weakness the intense pressure of judgment by the Almighty, whence springs so much social dynamism (cf. Abraham Lincoln).

Finally, the pope describes the views of those (like Richard Rorty, Arthur Schlesinger, and many others in this country) who argue that only agnosticism, relativism, and unbelief keep democracy safe: "Those who are convinced that they know the truth and firmly adhere to it are considered unreliable from a democratic point of view." Then, recalling recent experiences under Marxism, the pope turns the tables on them.

It must be observed in this regard that if there is no ultimate truth to guide and direct political activity, then ideas and convictions can easily be manipulated for reasons of power. As history demonstrates, a democracy without values easily turns into open or thinly disguised totalitarianism.

Centesimus Annus is a great encyclical, the greatest in a hundred years. It is the single best statement in our lifetime by the Catholic Church, or any other religious body, of the moral vision of a political economy such as that of the United States. That is why even Pope John Paul's diagnosis of serious faults in such systems is not offensive; his criticism hoists us on our own ideals. It is, so to speak, criticism "from within." It is as if the pope had written: "We hold these truths in faith: that all men are created equal and endowed by their Creator with certain unalienable rights, among which are the right to life . . ." and so on. Quite recognizable, that.

If in Vatican II Rome accepted ideas of religious liberty, in *Centesimus Annus* Rome has assimilated American ideas of economic liberty. Moreover, the pope has brought Rome to understand liberty as Americans do:

> *Confirm thy soul in self-control,*
> *Thy liberty in law.*

Look again at the Statue of Liberty: holding aloft the lamp of reason, in her other hand the Book of the Law, and bearing a visage as stern and purposive as that of any third-grade teacher in the history of our land.

17

Newness That Is Not New

JAMES V. SCHALL, S.J.

WHEN John Paul II issued *Sollicitudo Rei Socialis* (1987), I expressed concern that the Holy Father did not take sufficiently into account the nature and conditions of wealth production. The most pressing needs in this world, particularly poverty, have not been seen in their relation to wealth production. *Centesimus Annus* has largely remedied this disturbing lacuna. Let me remark briefly on four other aspects of this encyclical, however. Three of these give some cause for concern. On the questions of work, rights, and ecology, it seems to me, the Holy Father is not sufficiently aware of the potential problems and even dangers of his arguments, or the ways in which the central lines of his thought are likely to be misinterpreted or misunderstood. The fourth area, the specifically Christian contribution to modern social life, I take to be the deepest issue. It constitutes the essential "newness" of this document, precisely because it is not "new."

First, with regard to work, I admire the pope's effort to enhance the dignity of the worker as a person. Yet I find some problems with his notion of work compared to that put forth

James V. Schall, S.J., is a professor in the Department of Government at Georgetown University, and is a former member of the Pontifical Commission on Justice and Peace.

by Josef Pieper in *Leisure: The Basis of Culture*. Pieper is working out of the Greek distinction between things useful in themselves and things useful for other purposes. He is most concerned that intellectual effort and "work" not be simply identified. The Holy Father does not distinguish, within the world of work, between the servile and craft types of work, and the free or liberating types. The efforts to suggest that work is what most people do and that this is the normal way to support individuals and families, that each person's contribution to the world is important, and that not all work is the same, are valid enough. My concern is that not all higher human activities can be called "work."

Furthermore, the relation of work to the worker needs to be much more nuanced. The Holy Father has a marvelous sense of the human need to do something worthwhile and to get things done. Yet too much is made of work as important solely because it proceeds from the person of the worker. This can be a formula for stagnation, as if what counts is the worker, not the work, whatever it might be. What the work is in itself and what it contributes to the world are also of fundamental importance. The pope does emphasize, however, that excellence of work is now a major consideration.

Also, when it comes to voluntary worker organizations, such as unions, so beloved by the Holy Father in Poland, nothing is said of the actual record of modern labor except in praise. There is almost no hint here, though the pope has sometimes admitted it in other places, that unions present many problems by hindering productivity, interfering with worker freedom, engaging in corruption, and exerting undue political influence.

The Problem of "Rights"

Secondly, on the use of "rights" in papal documents: there is no indication that the pope is aware that this term has a very specific and problematic modern context. This encyclical has thrown its weight into the use of "rights" as the central pillar of its position, one that on its own grounds is able to appeal to everyone in an unequivocal sense. But is this so?

We find rights to many things praised in this document, and we find blame for the violation of them. Yet without much more clarification, the understanding of "rights" in most of modern political philosophy and law will continue to work against what the pope is driving at. In fact, he will be accused of "violating" rights when he asserts certain Catholic doctrines. (There is some allusion to this problem in #46, on the question of whether relativism can found a democracy.)

Depending on the sense we give to it, the concept of "rights" may or may not be a legitimate expression of Catholic social teaching, as the studies by Maritain, Simon, Strauss, McCoy, Finnis, Hittinger, Veatch, and others have shown. In today's usage, a right means a claim asserted against society by pure individual will. This will is limited only by another will, not by reason, as has traditionally been the case in Catholic and the best secular thought. There needs to be much more careful attention to the fact that the concept of "rights" is used today to promote issues and ways of life that are quite contrary to natural or Christian morality. The structure of the modern state, it is often thought, is intended to protect and promote these proliferating "rights." The Church itself is often seen to be hypocritical because it claims to uphold "rights" but denies those legislated by modern states or urged upon us by modern mores on the basis of popular will.

To speak about the right to religious freedom, or to property, or to the vote, or to a trial by jury in the same language that is used to demand the "right" to abortion or to deviant behavior is very confusing. I do not think it sufficient to say that the latter is merely an "abuse" of the word "rights," for this usage is the norm in modern philosophy. The Church is paying the price for this unclarity in its teaching. To continue it will pave the way for modernity, under the guise of absolute "rights," to become enshrined even in papal documents.

The third caution that I would direct at this encyclical has to do with its, to me, quite uncareful treatment of the notion of ecology and environment. In some sense, I suppose, the pope tries to guide this popular movement into areas in which it can be justified. But again, in all of the pope's recent remarks on this topic, I have never seen any clear awareness of the potential and actual anti-human and anti-Christian implications of an excessive enthusiasm for earth. Paul Johnson rightly, I think, has seen environmentalism as an offshoot of the same modernity from which both Marxism and liberalism arose, one again based on pure individual will, but this time bound up with the presumed primacy of nature over man ("Is Totalitarianism Dead?," *Crisis*, February 1989). In this view, environmentalism becomes one more form of totalitarianism enforced by the state.

"New Things" in Context

My final point concerns what I see as a renewed attention in *Centesimus Annus* to the fuller understanding of man made possible by revelation. This position stands in contrast to tendencies in social philosophy and in religious thought that would, like modernity itself, see Christianity as merely an aid to this-worldly development and progress. In his 1991 encyclical on missions, *Redemptoris Missio*, the Holy Father reiterated that, when all is said and done, Christians still have something to tell all men besides "make a better world." If anything, *Centesimus Annus* is a re-*new*-al of the Catholic social doctrine that points out the limits of the state and the limits of the world, not by opposing the worldly order but by indicating why it is not enough. The discussion of atheism, original sin, and socialism in this document is a reminder that man's true home is not on this earth, even under the best of all possible political regimes. It is characteristic of Thomism, for example, to maintain that the greatest deficiencies of human life are seen, not in the aberrations of history, but in what is lacking even when things are going well. This is what the Holy Father is getting at.

Consequently, we find in *Centesimus Annus* John Paul's endorsement of his predecessor Leo XIII's bedrock belief, expressed in *Rerum Novarum* ("Of New Things"), that "there can be *no genuine solution of the 'social question' apart from the Gospel,* and that the 'new things' can find in the Gospel the context for their correct understanding and the proper moral perspective for judgment on them" (#5; see also #58 and 59). Here, I think, John Paul is at his best. He is not preaching. He is not being unecumenical or unphilosophical. If there is any reason for modern intellectuals to dislike this pope, I think it lies here, in his insistence that modern philosophy, even at its best, does not have all the answers even for itself.

18

A Message Obscured by Static?

HERBERT SCHLOSSBERG

A T first, a surge of elation: the pope had issued an official statement that lays to rest the claim that socialism as a means for achieving justice is consistent with Roman Catholic teaching. Moreover, because the new encyclical was written in part to commemorate the centenary of *Rerum Novarum*, John Paul II was able to weave back and forth between past and present—between Leo XIII's warnings of the dangers of socialism and the miserable history of seventy years of "Real Socialism"—in a powerful way.

In light of that history and his profound understanding of it, John Paul's *intention* in this remarkable encyclical seems clear: he wants it to be understood, by those to whom he is speaking, that the free market (or, as he prefers, the "free economy") is the only economic system that can lead to justice. The pope has many qualifying things to say about the free economy, chiefly having to do with the cultural and legal boundaries that ought to discipline the market. But his intention, on this matter of economics, is clear, and I am happy to join the chorus of those who applaud it. The free economy is the system of choice for those who really care about justice.

Herbert Schlossberg is a project director of the Fieldstead Institute, Irvine, California.

But I see some problems. My chief concern is that the encyclical may not be "heard" according to the pope's intention. The reasons why it may not have to do with the recent history of our politics, and the recent history of our churches. The pope insists, rightly, that his is the voice of a pastor, not a politician. And yet this is a public document, addressed to "all men and women of good will." It will inevitably be used to buttress arguments for or against various public policy proposals. Does the encyclical protect itself against misinterpretation?

This is a matter of far more than academic interest to Protestants. The most significant fault lines among the churches today are not the "vertical" ones between formal ecclesiastical structures but the ideological ones that run through each church, aligning friends and foes irrespective of denominational flags. A small rumble in Roman Catholicism can become an earthquake where I live. Therefore it makes a great deal of difference how a document like *Centesimus Annus* is used. Can themes and phrases be extracted from it for purposes that contradict the pope's intention?

The Right to Own Property

Let me suggest some of the problem areas on this interpretive front. First, the question of property. Like his great predecessor Leo XIII, John Paul II defends the notion of private property. Indeed, *Centesimus Annus* seems far more sensitive than other Roman documents to the dangers posed to freedom and justice by the tendency of the modern state to assume an ever-larger role in the economy, thus whittling away at the rights (and opportunities) of private property owners.

On the other hand, the encyclical also stresses the theme of "the universal destination of the earth's goods." The origin of the phrase lies, of course, in the Genesis account of God's gift of the entire earth to humanity. But in today's ideological and political climate, where the Marxist hangover has yet to be fully cured, the phrase "universal destination of the earth's goods" will almost certainly be used as a kind of rhetorical life-jacket by those interested in saving otherwise dying systems.

The question, then, is, will "universal destination" be read as a general reminder of the social obligations incumbent on all property owners? Or will it be read as a papal endorsement of various pseudo-egalitarian and redistributionist schemes, whose empirical failures (precisely for poor people) are well known but whose allure remains powerful indeed?

The encyclical's teaching that private property is "illegitimate" if it is not used productively is also open to abuse. Who is qualified to judge whether property is employed productively enough? And who will right the alleged wrongs here? Does the encyclical set the stage for the political abrogation of the property rights that it elsewhere deems both just and essential?

The Role of the State

Second, there is the question of socialism, capitalism, and the state. On the one hand, the pope's denunciation of "Real Socialism" could hardly be clearer. And he does not suggest that the answer is a better socialism than the one imposed on Central and Eastern Europe. Socialism cannot be corrected by a new and improved model, because socialist theory is marred by a false anthropology. That mistake leads in turn to great human rights violations, and to further alienation. Socialism, according to John Paul II, is irredeemable, and there can be no compromise between Christianity and Marxism.

All well and good. But how does it serve the pope's intention here for the encyclical to question, at several points, the claim that capitalism is the only alternative to socialism? John

Paul II seems to endorse a capitalism in which law and culture direct the market toward truly human ends. But what are we then to make of a sentence like this: "We have seen that it is unacceptable to say that the defeat of so-called 'Real Socialism' leaves capitalism as the only model of economic organization."

Had the encyclical drawn the distinction between the free market and the special privileges for some that disfigure the market in all capitalist countries, the pope's plea that markets be freed from the politically imposed distortions and injustices that warp social and economic life would have been strengthened. But to leave an opening for some economic model other than capitalism may make it easier for governments to avoid doing what has to be done to free up the entrepreneurial energies that the pope celebrates.

Then there is what some will doubtless read as the pope's enthusiasm for the state in its task of "harmonizing and guiding development"—a reading that seems confirmed by the encyclical's willingness to concede a large role for the state in developing countries when private-sector entities are "too weak" or are "just getting under way and are not equal to the task at hand." True, John Paul says that such statist intervention must be brief; but those who have seized on these concessions as another ideological or political life-jacket may not read that far down the page.

Nor is there much reason to be sanguine about the pope's endorsement of global agencies to "oversee and direct the economy to the common good." Here again the principles of the encyclical seem undercut by some dubious applications. The pope insists that the damage done by "Real Socialism" can be repaired only by free citizens operating in a free economy. But why then do we need international controllers to supervise what the national controllers have botched? Are we supposed to think that though bureaucrats in Bucharest wrecked Romania, other bureaucrats in Brussels or New York can save the world?

There are other examples of this kind of thing, but perhaps the point has been made. *Centesimus Annus* could be a decisive force for good in the ongoing debate about the shape of the international economy, and the economies of states. But the great principles of freedom that the encyclical enunciates may be obscured by some static it generates at the level of practice and policy.

19

Away From the Zero-Sum View

ROBERT A. SIRICO, C.S.P.

To grasp the significance of *Centesimus Annus* requires a blend of two approaches. First, read it on its own merits. As objectively as possible, try to discern its thrust and priorities. Second, read it in the context of other social pronouncements by the Catholic teaching office over the past one hundred years and see what new themes and directions it initiates.

When read for itself, *Centesimus Annus* emerges as an uncompromising rejection of collectivism in its Marxist, Communist, socialist, and even welfare-statist manifestations. While the encyclical allows for a certain amount of intervention by the state in such areas as wage levels, social security, and unemployment insurance, it repeatedly expresses concern for observing the principle of subsidiarity, and warns against the effects of intervention both on the nation's economic prosperity and on individual persons' dignity and rights.

Centesimus Annus, then, indicates a decided preference for

Robert A. Sirico, C.S.P., is president of the Acton Institute for the Study of Religion and Liberty, in Grand Rapids, Michigan. This commentary appeared in the June 24, 1991, Special Supplement of *National Review* and is used by permission.

what it calls the "business economy," "market economy," or "free economy," rising out of a legal, ethical, and religious framework. While it rejects the notion that such a free economic system meets all human needs, it distinguishes the economic system from the ethical and cultural context in which it exists. In this way *Centesimus Annus* can criticize the excesses of materialism and consumerism and still endorse capitalism as essentially in accord with Christianity.

The second way of reading this encyclical reveals it as an even more dramatic document. When approached with an awareness of modern Catholic social thought, beginning with Leo XIII's *Rerum Novarum*, *Centesimus Annus* evidences the greatest depth of economic understanding and the most deliberate (and least critical) embrace of the system of free exchange on the part of Catholic teaching authority in one hundred years (and possibly since the Middle Ages). Moreover, it shows a modern appreciation for the dynamic nature of free exchange and the way in which wealth is produced.

When seen in this way, *Centesimus Annus* represents the beginnings of a shift away from the static zero-sum economic world view that led the Church to be suspicious of capitalism and to argue for wealth redistribution as the only moral response to poverty.

There are several dimensions to this new direction worth considering. The first is the clear difference in direction apparent when *Centesimus Annus* is read alongside the 1986 U.S. bishops' letter, *Economic Justice for All*. Where the pope virtually celebrates the virtues required for entrepreneurship, the American bishops look askance upon market activity and see it as redeemable only to the extent that it can be harnessed by government. The pope, even when he accepts the need for some state intervention, does so grudgingly, and goes to great lengths to limit intervention and to demand that it be withdrawn as soon as possible. The bishops' document, on the other hand, offers an energetic advocacy of expansive state intervention. The social-justice establishment has been left unprepared to consider social questions from within the framework the pope has constructed in *Centesimus Annus*. The materials that these ecclesiastical cognoscenti have produced show that they are unfamiliar with the Continental economic tradition represented by Wilhelm Röpke, Ludwig von Mises, F. A. Hayek, and Israel Kirzner, as well as the insights of the Virginia public-choice school and others.

A second implication of this encyclical is that entrepreneurs and capitalists have been invited in out of the moral cold to which they felt exiled in the past. The Holy Father affirms their basic vocation and role, even while he challenges them to look beyond the economic bottom line and consider the moral dimensions of their work.

A third implication is that this encyclical constitutes the epitaph for liberation and collectivist movements in terms of any official ecclesiastical legitimacy. The "Christian-Marxist dialogue" is dead, as even Gustavo Gutiérrez, father of liberation theology, has recently conceded.

Centesimus Annus indicates a turn toward authentic human liberty as a principle for social organization on the part of the world's largest Christian denomination. This encyclical will go down in history alongside Vatican II's *Dignitatis Humanae*, on religious liberty, as representing the impact the American experience has had on the teaching of the universal Church. What *Dignitatis Humanae* did to open the Church to the rights of conscience and religious liberty, *Centesimus Annus* will do to open the Church to a full and vigorous dialogue with the idea of economic liberty. It is an idea that began with Catholic scholarship as seen in the Scholastics; it is fitting that it should be retrieved by this pope.

20

An 'Evangelical' Impetus, A 'Catholic' Vision

MAX L. STACKHOUSE

THE first of the modern social encyclicals, Pope Leo XIII's *Rerum Novarum* (1891), was reserved in regard to democracy (the anti-clericalism of the French Revolution was well remembered) and opposed to socialism (whose anti-religious materialism was then still gaining ground). Still, Rome recognized that traditional, agricultural society was giving way to urban technological society. As the Protestant social gospel also claimed, human history was to be transformed. Succeeding social encyclicals—Pius XI's *Quadragesimo Anno* (1931), John XXIII's *Mater et Magistra* (1961) and *Pacem in Terris* (1963), Paul VI's *Populorum Progressio* (1967), and John Paul II's own *Laborem Exercens* (1981) and *Sollicitudo Rei Socialis* (1987)—raised in social ethics what Vatican II raised in matters of doctrine: hopes for a genuinely ecumenical future.

John Paul's *Centesimus Annus* is intended to commemorate, recall, assess, and extend this 100-year-old "new tradition." The pope wants not only to "manifest the true meaning of the

Max L. Stackhouse is Herbert Gezork Professor of Christian Social Ethics at Andover-Newton Theological School. This commentary is reprinted by permission from the May 29/June 5, 1991, issue of *The Christian Century*.

church's tradition" but also to apply it to "an analysis of some events of recent history."

Several features of this encyclical are immediately striking. To begin with, it repudiates socialism as analysis and as policy. It recognizes the radical social, historical, ethical, and theological significance of the anti-Communist, pro-democratic, and pro-market revolutions in Eastern Europe and in the Third World. For more than a century the primary dialogical partner for Christian social thought has been socialism. That dialogue is now over, for socialism, the pope argues in a half-dozen ways, has been exposed as false prophecy.

At the same time, the encyclical is sharply critical of the consumerism, possessiveness, and ecological damage (natural, social, and moral) that dehumanize life in non-socialist societies. It recognizes that these realities are what drove many to accept the false prophecy. The "preferential option for the poor," which grew out of the critique of non-socialist systems, is not to be forgotten. But it is to be manifested in action that helps "entire peoples which are presently . . . marginalized to enter into the sphere of economic and human development."

The keys to economic and human development identified here are not unfamiliar to Protestants. *Centesimus* speaks of "work" in terms that echo the "Protestant ethic" about which Max Weber wrote. It speaks also of private property in terms that sound like John Locke (whom some have called *the* Protestant social philosopher). And it manifests an appreciation of technological advances that was common in Protestant modernism—although praise for technology does not extend to abortion or to modern weaponry.

In economics the document distinguishes between "primitive capitalism" and "new capitalism," and the technological "new capitalism" is applauded in surprising ways. Indeed, the letter points out positive features of "profits," "markets," "self-interest," and "capital." Those who have come to believe that these features of modern economies are the causes of economic dislocation will have to struggle with this message, for the encyclical suggests that it is not the presence of these factors but the absence of them or lack of access to them that marginalizes individuals and peoples.

For people left out of modern modes of organizational culture and the new networks of skill that create wealth and evoke creativity, "economic development takes place over their heads." At the same time, those who do have access often find that, while the new capitalism produces plenty, it does not by itself overcome forms of alienation in which persons are distant from God, truth, and communion with others. The implications of both points for ministry and mission are vast.

The Associational Person

Such analysis turns out to be rooted in a more general theory of society. John Paul affirms and extends Leo's claim about a "natural human right to form private associations"— families, unions, firms, professional groups, and the like—that "precedes" a person's involvements in political society. This claim is remarkable on three counts.

First, it sees human rights as a part of Christian teaching. While that idea is not new, it has come under sharp criticism during recent decades both from radical theologies that view human rights as bourgeois idealism and from conservative forms of communitarian ethics that doubt the existence of any tradition- or context-transcending principles.

Second, it emphasizes the importance of intentional or voluntary societies, an idea frequently criticized by all who claim that we best understand humanity in terms of natural groups. On the one hand, this view modifies natural-law theories that are embedded in static conceptions of social order, for it recognizes that some social and cultural artifacts are morally indispensable. On the other hand, it modulates current notions of "solidarity," which is here interpreted in terms of "friendship," "charity," and "civilization" marked by love. It thus stands in contrast to every exclusive affirmation of class, gender, and national or ethnic identity.

Third, the argument about the right of association appears to reinforce a free-church Protestant contention. Those forms of Protestantism that have opposed centralized regimes and established religion have long claimed that people have the right to organize independently of the Caesars, the Herods, and the high priests of the world. In fact, this was often regarded as the central organizational issue of the New Testament, suppressed by the medieval church. Whether the Roman Catholic Church is ready for all the implications of this emphasis is yet to be seen.

Society Before the State

Yet the encyclical clearly says that society is prior to politics. The pope writes that while the defenseless and the poor have special claims to protection by the government, the state's intervention is to be "instrumental," "limited," and "as brief as possible." To put it another way, sociality and anthropology are prior to political economics.

But the logic of the general theory of society goes even deeper: to get our view of sociality and anthropology straight, we have to get our theology straight. It is here that some of the greatest differences between the encyclical and key currents of modern thought emerge. The encyclical affirms that the "very worst evils" arise out of a denial of truth in the objective sense. "If there is no transcendent truth . . . there is no sure principle for guaranteeing just relations between people," or even for recognizing the dignity of the human person.

On the basis of the recognition that all human beings stand under transcendent truth, democracy is affirmed more fully than in any other encyclical in Catholic history. Echoes of the Declaration of Independence, as invoked by John Courtney

Murray a generation ago—"We hold these truths to be self-evident . . ."—resound in sentence after sentence. Speaking explicitly against the "claim that agnosticism and skeptical relativism are the philosophy and the basic attitude which correspond to democratic forms of political life," this document claims that "authentic democracy is possible only in a state ruled by law and on the basis of a correct conception of the human person." And these depend, above all, on what Murray and many since him have called "public theology." The issues at this level are not only philosophical or ethical but explicitly theological—and in principle accessible to all.

In this context, the encyclical speaks of "globalization." The public that is addressed is humanity, and not only Catholics or Christians and certainly not only those influenced by Western traditions. The question is the relationship of the knowledge of God to the construction of a civilization of worldwide interdependence.

Many today are persuaded that we cannot speak about such matters reliably. We can only try to be faithful by telling our faith story in a particular communion, by attempting to come to a personal relationship with God, and by trying to live out the Gospel in our daily lives. Surely such fidelity is not false: the "evangelical" accent has always been a part of authentic Christian witness. Others are convinced that the living God is Lord over the whole earth and the whole of history, and that we are most faithful when we seek to develop those forms of theology and ethics that can interpret and address the great systems of technology, economics, politics, and law whereby humanity is bound together in a global civilization. This "catholic" accent has also always been part of authentic Christian witness.

In the past a chief Protestant criticism of the Roman Catholic tradition was, not only that it had lost its evangelical accent, but that it became so Roman it had lost its catholicity. This charge is more difficult to make after this century of encyclicals, and especially after *Centesimus*. Ecumenical Protestants often wrestle with questions of inclusiveness and pluralism that neither evangelicals nor Catholics face directly. Our witness would be enriched by both the evangelical impetus and the catholic vision present in this encyclical.

21

A View From the Ruins

JOZEF TISCHNER

NATIONS that have endured the historical experiment of Communism, lured by the promise of "progress," are horrified to discover that they are now surrounded on all sides by ruins—ruined economies, ruined state institutions, ruined people. The destruction of private property and the devastation of economic life as an aftermath of uncritical faith in the omnipotence of a planned economy are most striking. But hand in hand with economic disintegration goes the disintegration of political life—an outcome of totalitarianism.

The breakdown of the economy and the polity places great demands upon both those who were victims and those who were executors of the system. Totalitarian rule consists in subordination and creates subordinates. After its fall, old habits do not disappear. You can see inscriptions on city walls in Poland saying "Commies—come back." Their authors are people of whom the liberalization of the economy and politics demands something they are incapable of—a personal responsibility for their own actions. Communism's material ravages

---

Jozef Tischner is a professor on the philosophy faculty of the Papal Theological Academy in Krakow. His comments, translated by Beata Wojnika, appeared in the June 24, 1991, Special Supplement of *National Review* and are used by permission.

are small compared with the devastation of the internal, spiritual world of the individual.

John Paul II is one of the very few people in the West to recognize fully the extent of the devastation resulting from Communism, not only in economics and politics but primarily within man himself. He knows it is not enough to pull down the external structures of Communism; the totalitarian mentality must also be overcome in each human being.

I myself am an inhabitant of a ruined land. With so many others I ask, Why did Communism fall? I understand the breakdown of the economy, I understand the ineffectiveness of the bureaucracy. But the real reason lies elsewhere: rebellious man. Freedom was born in an enslaved world. Free people overthrew Communism. Therefore, I find the following passage of the encyclical particularly important:

> The fundamental error of socialism is anthropological in nature. Socialism considers the individual person simply as an element, a molecule within the social organism, so that the good of the individual is completely subordinated to the functioning of the socio-economic mechanism. Socialism also maintains that the well-being of the individual can be realized without reference to his free choice, to the unique and exclusive responsibility which he exercises in the face of good or evil.

And, at a different point: "Not only is it wrong from the ethical point of view to disregard human nature, which is made for freedom, but in practice it is impossible to do so." Socialism's "anthropological mistake" is the encyclical's recurring theme. While criticizing the Communist concept of man, the encyclical reminds us of the Christian vision: "Indeed, it is through the free gift of self that man truly finds himself." This is not a theoretical abstraction. In a world ruled by Communists there appeared heroes—overthrowing Communism. It is not a "man with growing needs," not a "consuming man" who has achieved this historical aim, but a responsibly free man.

Economic Instruction

In addition to diagnosing Communism's failure, one who, like me, lives among post-Communist ruins expected the encyclical to instruct him in two basic fields: the economy and political life.

Regarding the economy: Marxist criticisms of the free market, criticisms of profit and private ownership, are still fresh in our mind. In social consciousness there still live unrealistic myths about the functioning of a market economy—many dream of capitalist wealth without the capitalist effort. That's why a clear and comprehensive moral legitimation of the basic principles of a liberal economy is of the utmost importance. As the encyclical states: "It would appear that, on the level of individual nations and of international relations, *the free market* is the most efficient instrument for utilizing resources and effectively responding to needs."

This legitimation is not in contradiction to what the author says about the threat of "alienation" of labor. John Paul II gives a new meaning to the notion of "alienation," used and abused by Marxists: it consists of a "reversal of relations between means and aims." Man is not for the economy, but the economy for man.

Political Instruction

As regards politics, the basic issue is restructuring the state. The assumptions John Paul II makes in this respect are vital. He defends the concept of a "legally governed country," "appreciates democracy," acknowledges "the principle of subsidiarity" as the basis of state operation, and reminds the state of its moral obligation to intervene in economic life, particularly regarding poverty, and in cultural life. He does not share the view that the philosophy of a democratic state should be "agnosticism and skeptical relativity"; rather it should be "an appropriate concept of the human being." The state should protect human rights. John Paul II juxtaposes the fallen totalitarian state to a state under the "rule of law," with a strong ethical element. In such a state there is a place for the Church, because it operates on the principle of "respecting freedom."

Does this imply that all questions have been answered? The architects of new states in the post-Communist era must face the problem of how state legislation, which must be binding upon everyone, should be harmonized with the principles and norms of ethical systems that, in a pluralistic society, are diverse and often contradictory. In Poland, these are the grounds for debates about such matters as the introduction of religion into schools, abortion, contraception, and the "attitudes" of state officials.

The encyclical is particularly important for the newly liberated countries, whose people remember Communism very vividly. It teaches responsibility. For Poles it is all the more important, as it speaks about Poland, Solidarity, a peaceful struggle that "required a presence of mind, restraint, suffering, and sacrifice." John Paul II attributes special meaning to the Polish events. I wonder if the time has come to compare what took place in Poland with the French Revolution, and to consider whether what was initiated—in a certain sense—by the earlier revolution was not halted by the Polish "revolution," and whether the success of overthrowing Communism is comparable to the success of overthrowing feudalism.

Epilogue

The Importance of What's Absent

ROBERT ROYAL

I N good Trinitarian fashion, responses to a papal encyclical usually fall into three categories, one positive and two negative. First, readers who generally like what they find will praise the encyclical because of one or more of its parts—the parts that confirm what they already believe. Readers who dislike the encyclical divide into the second and third categories: some will criticize it for what it says, others for what it fails to say, but in either case, also on grounds of previously held beliefs.

Only once in a very great while, almost too rare even to mention, does a reader sit down, peruse an encyclical, and have some sort of conversion experience. For most people, an encyclical is just one more text to read and criticize rather than a text that reads and criticizes us.

Yet there is another possible way of evaluating a papal

Robert Royal is vice president for research and Olin Fellow in Religion and Society at the Ethics and Public Policy Center. He has contributed to and edited several books, including (with George Weigel) *A Century of Catholic Social Thought* and (with Virgil Nemoianu) *The Hospitable Canon: Essays on Literary Play, Scholarly Choice, and Popular Pressures.*

encyclical: a positive response to it for things it does *not* say. At first blush, this *theologia negativa* of encyclicals may seem merely one more attempt to foist on the pope and on the teaching authority of the Roman Catholic Church positions that neither explicitly holds. But in fact we might fruitfully follow the lead of some postmodern theorists (generally a very non-religious bunch) and recognize that some of the strongest and most controlling elements in a text may be those that exist only outside it, or on its margins, as basic assumptions. In line with some recent hermeneutics, a reading of *Centesimus Annus* for some of the things that are rightly and edifyingly *absent* from it should lead us to consider what may lie unexamined in what we believe and who we are.

A Modest Historiography

To begin with, this document does not give even the slightest hint of grounds for belief in grand historical systems of any stripe. The collapse of Marxism and the parallel general discrediting of total or "scientific" theories of history (everything from Vico and Hegel to Spengler and Toynbee now seems far less plausible than it did pre-1989) return us to a theological truth concealed within the assumptions of the papal text. While the Bible is *the* history-creating book, in the sense that its unfinished story of Creation-Fall-Salvation sets up unilinear human time, Sacred Scripture gives us no detailed roadmap of the human future in this world. Archaic societies, with their cyclical patterns of foundation, departure, and return to original form, know the future because they know the past. Western societies, whose sense of time largely derives from the Bible, have, instead, that at times terrifying, at times promising uncertainty known as history. The Christian future is an open field.

In the afterglow of 1989, scientific theories of history look more and more like all-too-human attempts to take control of

God's time by closing off human liberties. Those theories claimed to be paths of emancipation, but in fact turned more often into flights from freedom into various reductivist determinisms and historical "laws." The Catholic Church has never been much taken with supposedly scientific explanations of human life. Contrary to much nineteenth-century expectation, the Church and *Centesimus Annus* as we approach the end of the second Christian millennium reflect a far more open and welcoming vision of the future and of human liberty than do many secular pundits.

Of course, a Christian must always approach the future with "fear and trembling" (properly understood); but John Paul II strikes the right note when he describes this encyclical as an invitation to look toward the future since "we can already glimpse the Third Millennium of the Christian era, so filled with uncertainties but also with promises—uncertainties and promises which speak to our imagination and creativity, and which reawaken our responsibility." In other words, while we may dimly glimpse paths toward better forms of social and political organization than what we have, creating them depends on often frail and always fallen human individuals. Not only does such a theological vision deny the presumption that predicted an ideal future in which the state would simply wither away; it also warns us against assuming that once we establish democracy or markets or some other mere mechanism of public life, progress will be automatic. There might even be—*mirabile dictu*—regression on some fronts. The human future, as always, depends on the quality of human intelligence, imagination, and choice—a truism worth reasserting in the wake of theories that denied it.

Proper Generalities

Many people continue to criticize the Church's social teaching for what they see as its over-reliance on generalities of this sort and a failure to address specific political and economic issues. While the charge is true—the Church does, for the most part, stick with generalities, it only rarely feels called upon to address specific issues—the judgment that the lack of specifics constitutes a drawback is simply wrong. The Church, we should not need to be reminded, is not a school of foreign service, political philosophy, economics, or business administration. Neither is it the United Nations or some international Department of State. Its primary concern is to emphasize theological truths that cannot be ignored without grave human peril in the public realm.

While *Centesimus Annus* aims at providing pastoral guidance about some of the events of recent history, it erects a barrier against theocratic temptations, even subtle ones, by its insistence in several places that passing definitive judgments on complex social issues "does not fall within the Magisterium's specific domain." Nevertheless, the Church does point out errors that lie within its specific competence, errors such as false views of man and history. This boundary-setting function has—or may have—significant real-world consequences. For instance, John Paul commends his predecessor Leo XIII for his prescience in noting, before any government had yet become officially socialist, that if socialist solutions were implemented, "the working man himself would be among the first to suffer." Millions of Polish, Russian, Czechoslovak, and other workers have paid the price for their compatriots' failure to heed this warning.

Or take another example: It is one of the principal tenets of Catholic social teaching that all people are equally a part of society and that no class is either a privileged vanguard or an absolute enemy. Individual equality, however, does not mean that a society will not be articulated into different strata. In fact, the Church teaches that this articulation works, at its best, for the common good. The poor are more vulnerable than others, however, and need particular attention in the laws. John Paul calls this attention "solidarity" and notes that Leo XIII, echoing an Aristotelian concept, used the term "friendship" for the same idea, which is "one of the fundamental principles of the Christian view of social and political organization." Without specifying what form that special concern for the poor should take (in fact, for the first time in a Vatican document we are warned about the potential disincentives created by social services and the dangers of an irresponsible welfare bureaucracy), the encyclical points out the continued relevance of the principle of solidarity. Such ways of approaching social issues "are affirmations which do not depend on a specific notion of the State or a particular political theory." The Church's proper role is to expound the essential elements of a political theology rather than to spell out the ideal regime.

Political Agnosticism

Often, the very people who would most resent Catholic political pretensions take their absence as a sign of intellectual weakness or irrelevance. We might usefully recall here George Bernard Shaw's weighing of the relative claims of authority by the pope and by the world in the preface to *Saint Joan:*

> Compared to our infallible democracies, our infallible medical councils, our infallible astronomers, our infallible judges, and our infallible parliaments, the Pope is on his knees in the dust confessing his ignorance before the throne of God, asking only that as to certain historic matters on which he clearly has more sources of information open to him than anyone else, his decision shall be taken as final.

In politics, the Catholic Church is properly agnostic on many specific issues, while secular analysts are far more dogmatic exponents of political creeds.

Specifically, some Western commentators (even some within this volume) find John Paul's qualified support for democracy and capitalism to be welcome ammunition against residual socialist impulses inside and outside the Church; but they claim that the encyclical does not go anywhere near far enough in supporting these political and economic victors of the modern world. Democracy and capitalism, however, are not theological dogmas, though each honors some views of human nature—particularly respect for the intellect, imagination, and will—that accord well with Catholic teaching. The encyclical adopts a pragmatic stance towards both. Nevertheless, one of the strongest, if indirect, signs of the pervasive, provisional acceptance of democratic capitalism is that nowhere do crypto-Marxist allusions to "late" capitalism (still quite common in socialist analyses with their assumed knowledge of a future collapse of the capitalist order) enter this clear-eyed text. If anything, the pope hopes for a future in which more countries will find their way to a juridically framed capitalism. But he properly says (repeating an insight of Aristotle's) that each country, while respecting certain universal truths, must decide the shape of its institutions based on its own culture and history.

In addition to its reticence about individual nations, the encyclical refrains from detailed analyses of how the international order should be shaped. That there must be a world order that allows all nations access to the First World economy and that seeks to care for those who cannot help themselves almost goes without saying. But the big change is that all the grand and dangerously simple-minded schemes for a New International Economic Order, New Global Information Order, and other Marxist-inspired fantasies (some of which found tacit acceptance in earlier encyclicals, such as *Populorum Progressio*) are no longer even given notice. Democracies and markets will have to arrive at beneficial international arrangements by free decisions in this new dispensation.

Over the centuries, the Church has been forced to co-exist (sometimes with great discomfort, to put it mildly) with regimes that were neither democratic nor capitalist, and it knows it may have to do so again. For all their achievements, both democracy and capitalism are, after all, human creations, and however much they may express our best thought and practice at present, in the future they may be superseded by developments that will make our current conceptions of them as outmoded as feudalism or bimetallism. To say this does not take anything away from their value to us now. All earthly kingdoms fall short of the one true kingdom, and that realization is fruitful in this world because it makes us wary, and also more modest in our expectations of what politics and economics can do.

Transhistorical Truths

In spite of the encyclical's reticence about the meaning of history, one of the key Christian theological concepts about public life puts in a brief appearance in *Centesimus Annus:* the notion of Divine Providence. The great father of speculation about the role of Providence in history is, of course, Saint Augustine. Writing in the waning years of the Roman *imperium*, Augustine gratefully acknowledged the providential union of diverse peoples under that system, which made it possible for the Gospel to spread across ethnic and geographical borders. Christ had appeared in "the fullness of time," when what was basically the known world around the Mediterranean could receive his message *en bloc*. Subsequent Christian thinkers, following in Augustine's footsteps, have tried to discern the diverse workings of the divine will in the Dark Ages, the High Middle Ages, the Renaissance, and so on.

Of course, all such assertions are by their very nature speculations. We do not fully understand God's action in history. But the sudden collapse of the Communist world, the dismantling of the Berlin Wall shortly after the first openings of freedom, and the preternaturally peaceful revolutions in the former Eastern bloc have been read by the Vatican (and some other observers) as so miraculous, after decades of unwavering totalitarianism, that they suggest a direct intervention of Providence in history. As a pre-1989 Polish joke put it somewhat prophetically: "There are only two potential solutions for the crisis in Poland, one realistic and one miraculous. The realistic solution would be for the Virgin Mary to reappear at Czestochowa and convert the entire nation. The miraculous solution would be for the Communist government to allow real reform."

The encyclical emphasizes its attempt to read the "new things" of the present through a lens largely shaped by the events of 1989. While many have pointed out the political, economic, and social dimensions of such a reading, we would also do well to keep in mind the longer-term, providential dimension, which serves as a subtext. John Paul does not make any definitive claims about God's plans for the human future, but he is right to underscore the presence of what surely should be called a new spirit in the world.

The "modern" period, stretching, say, from the seventeenth century to the last few decades, brought with it enormous increases in human wealth, well-being, and liberty, at least in the developed world. There are several signs, allowing for the somewhat vague way that we divide history into generalized compartments, that this period may now be coming to an end. The very fact that the terms "postmodern," "postindustrial," and "post–Cold War" are in widespread use (and, for good and for ill, provoke acrimonious debates over their natures) should alert us to some deep shift in our self-understanding. The beginning of the Third Christian Millennium, as the encyclical points out, may be of more than mere chronological significance. We may be at the start of a whole new phase of thinking about the human person.

A Fruitful Marriage of New and Old

John Paul was a student and exponent of modern philosophy long before his assumption of the papal office, of course, and all his writing on human nature has been marked by a fruitful exchange between traditional approaches to defining the human person and the dynamic concepts of human creativity and development that he has gleaned from existentialism and phenomenology. Both Scholastic and modern currents of thought regard man as something other and richer than the self-transparent, rational being described by most humanist philosophers of the last few centuries. It is probably inevitable that, when Christian anthropological concepts appear in a social analysis such as the encyclical, their profound roots in the *mysterium fidei* will be attenuated. But it also is perhaps one of the deepest assumptions of current papal thinking that these truths about man are the reason Marxism failed and are the basis for a renewed world in the future: as the pope puts it, "the main thread and, in a certain sense, the guiding principle of Pope Leo's Encyclical, and of all of the Church's social doctrine, is a correct view of the human person."

We should be clear what these truths about the human person entail. In his dense phenomenological treatise *The Acting Person*, and in other writings, John Paul has spelled out his reasons for believing that to argue that there is a human nature and that we know what it is does not yield a deterministic or potentially totalitarian theory of human life. Fears of such negative consequences have been a staple of all poststructuralist and analytic philosophies of recent creation.

Nor does a Christian view of human nature, the pope shows, give anyone an absolutely privileged Archimedean point of social analysis. Marxists may speak glibly of false consciousness and bourgeois reality, but the Church cannot. For a Christian anthropology, human intellect and will can never simply be false consciousness and mistaken praxis. The person always bears a transcendent value, whether as knower or as doer. The missionary performing charitable works, for example, may not fully understand the causes of poverty and how to alleviate them, but when he recognizes suffering and responds to it, he is not in false consciousness. Where gross public evils exist, we all have responsibilities to correct them. But one of the lessons to be drawn from the Marxist catastrophe is that no body of truths should be allowed to override the basic human rights and transcendent dimension of the people. Even those crippled by evil systems have human dignity and access to truth, and should have a say in their own futures.

This is worlds away from the theorist's usual assumption of intellectual superiority. In fact, one of the *explicit* theological messages of the encyclical is that, for all his achievements, man cannot save himself. Human achievements always have unintended side effects and are crippled by the weaknesses and blind spots of the very people who bring them about. While not abandoning the concept of human effort, the encyclical also directs our attention elsewhere:

> In order that the demands of justice may be met, and attempts to achieve this goal may succeed, what is needed is the gift of grace, a gift which comes from God. Grace, in cooperation with human freedom, constitutes that mysterious presence of God in history which is Providence. . . . In order better to incarnate the one truth about man in different and constantly changing social, economic, and political contexts, this teaching enters into dialogue with the various disciplines concerned with man. It assimilates what these disciplines have to contribute, and helps them to open themselves to a broader horizon, aimed at serving the individual person who is acknowledged and loved in the fullness of his or her vocation.

This may strike some non-Catholic, and even some Catholic, readers as the usual theological trump card. But for many who suffered under closed atheistic systems, the transcendent window beyond every human science has practical value. Even Communist theorists came close to such an insight in the waning years of the Soviet bloc. One group in Czechoslovakia, for example, noting the aridity of several fields under scientific atheism, began speaking about God as a useful "ultimate horizon" for opening up human disciplines that had become either sclerotic or too closed in on their own portions of truth.

Such insights were also echoed by Václav Havel, a thinker and doer who, though not a practicing Catholic, anticipates many facets of *Centesimus Annus* in his writing. In his letters from prison to his wife Olga he wrote: "The tragedy of modern man is not that he knows less and less about the meaning of his own life, but that it bothers him less and less." Havel warned against a narrowing of vision to the merely utilitarian, however humane, and tried to wake his fellow countrymen to the value—in this life—of the kinds of ultimate horizons emphasized in papal thought.

True Freedom

Some Westerners bridle at invocations of ultimate truths, such as the pope's remarks that "*obedience to the truth* about God and man is the first condition of freedom," and that "freedom attains its full development only by accepting the truth." To Western ears, these sound like muffled claims for a theological definition of the public realm. If John Paul were advocating a specific state structure or mandatory adherence to a creed, such fears might be justified. But to read these phrases in that fashion is to get the theological message of the encyclical precisely backwards. Just as the American Founders felt it necessary to proclaim certain truths as self-evident, and to declare that all men had been endowed by their Creator with certain inalienable rights, so does John Paul remind us that the concrete truth about reality sets us free.

In pluralistic societies, such assertions may seem naïve, or even incredible. But John Paul is not saying that we must agree about political issues, or a certain abstract philosophy, or the immediate choices for the future. He is saying that without certain beliefs about man and society we not only are not free—we *cannot* be free. What we call freedom, under such circumstances, conceals a bondage to some human creation that is less than the full destiny of man. In his Farewell Address, George Washington argued in a similar vein: "Virtue or morality . . . is a natural spring of popular government. . . . Reason and experience both forbid us to expect that national morality can prevail in exclusion of religious principle."

At the very least, *Centesimus Annus* should lead us to acknowledge that the role of theology in world politics is due for a revaluation, particularly as we are thinking about new worldly orders. We know that people are moved mightily—in Eastern and Central Europe, in the Middle East, in South Africa, in Tibet, to name only a few obvious places—by religious views that have more and more acquired a worldly dimension. (After the Communist invasion of his country, even the Dalai Lama, a leader of a relatively quietistic religion, came to recognize the essential link between religious belief and concrete public action.) While practitioners of *Realpolitik* may minimize the influence of religion, it continues to be a major force in the world, particularly where it confronts political evils.

In this striking document, John Paul has reminded us, not only of the specifics of Catholic social doctrine, but of the ineradicable spiritual dimension of man that sooner or later, as became clear in 1989, will not be denied. The large absence of that theological dimension in most of our public deliberations points, as postmodernism suggests absences often do, to something that needs attention not only from our political and economic institutions but from each of us.

Index of Names